FROM THE CALTON TO CATALONIA

A play about the Scots who fought Franco

FROM THE CALTON TO CATALONIA

A play about the Scots who fought Franco

John Maley
and
Willy Maley

GLASGOW'S INDEPENDENT RADICAL BOOKSHOP

© John Maley and Willy Maley

From The Calton To Catalonia - John Maley and Willy Maley
First published 1992 by Glasgow City Libraries

This second edition published in 2014 by **Calton Books**, 159 London Road, Glasgow G1 5BX, Scotland

www.calton-books.co.uk

ISBN 978-0-9928983-0-4 (Paperback)

Printed by Clydeside Press, Glasgow

Cover by Stephen Cameron

Distribution AK Press & Distribution, 33 Tower Street Edinburgh EH6 7BN mailto:ak@akedin.demon.co.uk

Fighting Fascism 75 years Down the Line
John Maley and Willy Maley

It's 75 years since the end of the Spanish Civil War, and 25 years since we first sat down to think about a play commemorating those Scottish volunteers for liberty who engaged in the struggle against fascism. As sons of one of the Scots who fought Franco we wanted to celebrate the commitment of men like James Maley (1908-2007).

Glasgow has few public monuments commemorating its radical history. The statue of La Pasionaria at Custom House Quay on Clyde Street is a striking exception. It is fitting that such a tribute to the astonishing contribution made by its citizens to the anti-fascist struggle in Spain should take the shape of the woman from the Basque country, Dolores Ibarruri, known universally as "La Pasionaria" ("The Passion Flower") for her fiery rhetoric, which inspired many of those who made the journey across the Pyrenees. Ibarruri was a founding figure in the Spanish Communist Party, and her statue is one of the most prominent celebrations of Red Clydeside and of the cause of socialism in Scotland. It is also a landmark for the Left and a clear marker of Scottish internationalism and anti-fascism, standing out against the skyline that many Scottish volunteers for liberty would never see again.

Paul Preston, the leading authority on the Spanish Civil War, has written of Ibarruri: "In both her private life and in the political arena, the essential characteristics of Pasionaria were empathy with the sufferings of others, a fierce determination to correct injustice, strength, realism, flexibility, and, as the years passed, a touch of cynicism and an obsession with the unity of the Spanish

Communist party."[1] The plaque on the Clydeside statue salutes "the courage of those men and women who went to Spain to fight Fascism 1936-39", and remembers the sixty-five Glaswegians who died defending democracy. It repeats a famous phrase from a speech by La Pasionaria broadcast on the 3rd of September 1936: "Better to die on your feet than to live forever on your knees."

Those words moved our father, James Maley, to go to Spain. James was a Calton Republican, brought up in Stevenson Street and educated at St Alphonsus. He was also member of the International Brigades. Born in Glasgow's East End in 1908, he joined the Communist Party in February 1932, becoming a speaker and tutor for the Party. He used to carry his collapsible platform, from Glasgow Green to Govan Cross, wherever there were meetings. He joined the Territorial Army in 1934 and learned how to use a rifle.

Of 40,000 international volunteers from fifty-three countries, 2,100 were British, 550 were from Scotland, and around half of those hailed from Glasgow. 65 from Glasgow died, 134 from Scotland altogether. It's hard to understand how Scotland could make such a contribution without understanding the nature of Scottish radical politics at the beginning of the twentieth century. What's been called a 'lost left' – Guy Aldred, James Connolly, John Maclean, John Wheatley, and a host of other forgotten heroes – and a lost left with particular revolutionary, Irish and republican interests and commitments, emerged from the slums of Glasgow and Edinburgh, and from the shipyards, coalfields and factories of Scotland.

---

[1]. *Paul Preston, 'La Pasionaria', 66th Marx Memorial Lecture, Bulletin of the Marx Memorial Library 130 (1999), p. 8.*

On Thursday 31st December 1936, James Maley left from George Square in Glasgow on one of three packed double-decker buses bound for London, so packed there were men standing. By then he was living at 500 Shettleston Road, and he saw a few familiar faces on the bus. Glasgow's East End was the kind of community that raised a lot of radicals, rebels, and republicans. James Maley was part of the machine-gun company, Number 2 Company, led by Harold Fry, one of four companies in the British Battalion. The company spent that first night learning how to operate the Russian water-cooled Maxim machine-gun. The company engaged in heavy fighting over the weekend of 12th and 13th February 1937. The Battle of Jarama was a costly encounter. Half the 500-strong British Battalion were killed or wounded. Only 125 of the 400 members of the rifle companies survived. It was particularly costly for the machine gun company.

The British Battalion were outnumbered three to one, fighting alongside the Dimitrov Battalion – made up of Greeks and others from the Balkans, one of whose commanders was later better known as Marshall Tito – and the Abraham Lincoln Battalion. The British Battalion was also known as the "Saklatvala Battalion", after Shapurji Saklatvala, the British Indian who became the first Communist MP (on a Labour ticket) for Battersea North in 1922, and later stood unsuccessfully for Glasgow Shettleston, James Maley's constituency, in 1930. Saklatvala had died in January 1936 but as an internationalist his name resonated with the International Brigades.

As one member of the machine gun company, Tommy Bloomfield, later recalled: "Of our 120 men, three had gone back for ammo, we had 29 survivors, and the rest were killed". Those 29 survivors, including my father, were captured on the 13th of February while covering the retreat on "Suicide Hill". Phil Elias from Leeds was shot when he reached into his pocket for a cigarette (which he had asked to do and had the okay for). Ted Dickenson, second-in-command, was also shot, because he was recognised as an officer. That left twenty-seven men, who had their thumbs tied with telephone wire and were forced along on foot behind enemy lines by Moorish cavalry. They were taken to a wee place called Talavera De La Reina, where they were put in 3 cells, nine men to a cell, and finally, in the middle of May, to the Model Prison at Salamanca, where they were charged with 'aiding military rebellion'. The day they arrived at Salamanca 37 Spaniards were executed as well as German and Russian International Brigaders.

James Maley was older than most of his comrades. He turned twenty-nine on the 19th February 1937. During interrogations, Bert 'Yank' Levy, a Canadian, advised the men to answer truthfully but slyly. Why were they in Spain? To do a job of work. When would they leave? When the job was done. Things improved. The first day the prisoners got 'one ration and two

Jarama captives, February 1937 including author's father James Maley, front row, first right.

bashings'. The second day they got 'two rations and one bashing'. The bashings came from Germans and Moors. Harold Fry and Jimmy Rutherford were sentenced to death, the others to 20 years.

Luckily, the Italian defeat at Guadalajara in March made possible a prisoner exchange, and the Jarama captives were released, crossing the border into France on 30th May 1937. James Maley came home and continued to speak on his soapbox. Harold Fry did go back to Spain, the day before his son was born. Fry was appointed Commander of the British Battalion on 29th September 1937, and died at the Ebro on 13th October. Jimmy Rutherford went back too, and was executed by firing squad on 24 May 1938, aged 20.

A lot of Scots were on the soapbox in the 1930s, with Catholic denunciations of Communism going hand-in-hand with Irish Republican and socialist denunciations of the Church's stance. The East End of Glasgow was a particular crucible of contention, drawing as it did great support for Communists, anarchists and ILP-ers. John McGovern, Independent Labour Party MP for Shettleston, went to Spain in November 1936 and wrote a pamphlet called Why Bishops Back Franco. McGovern angered his Catholic constituents with his attacks on the Church's stance on Spain. As a Catholic radical McGovern took issue with right-wing Catholics. Likewise, James Maley hated anti-Catholic prejudice, but he hated fascist Catholics even more. Spain was a deeply divisive issue. The Ancient Order of Hibernians had come out against the Spanish Republic and in support of the fascists in August 1936. The Catholic Union of Scotland was loudly pro-Franco. Catholic supporters of Franco heckled Willie Gallacher, Communist MP for West Fife at meetings in his constituency. There were tensions between British and Irish volunteers in Spain because some British volunteers had served in the British army in Ireland during the war of independence. This was sorted out through the intervention of Frank Ryan, a leader in the IRA and a major in the XVth International Brigade, though some Irish volunteers chose to join the Abraham Lincoln Brigade rather than the British.

The son of an Irish navvy and a Glaswegian hawker, James Maley's politics were forged on Red Clydeside – forged too at Parkhead Forge, where he worked on his return from Spain. Interestingly, even after evidence of covert blacklisting of men who fought in Spain was produced, our father put down his own experiences of being passed over for work after the war to anti-Catholicism. So he was a Red to the Catholic Church and a Fenian to the bigots.

The Spanish Civil War is the war of the activist, the idealist, the "poets' war", but also a war of memory, a time of slogans written in blood: "No Pasaran!" The defiant statue of La Pasionaria gazing across the Clyde sums up the spirit of the age: "Better to die on your feet than to live forever on your knees". Spain remains a touchstone topic for the British Left, its finest hour, and yet also the place where the seeds of nostalgia, bitterness and failure were sown. The British Left has been less inclined in recent years to celebrate the mass action of the 1920s and 1930s. The Rent Strikes, the Unemployed Workers Movement, the Hunger Marches, these are in danger of being forgotten now.

James Maley was never one for harping on the past, and as an internationalist he certainly wasn't one for putting things into national boxes, but he did believe that real citizenship meant an end to empire and monarchy. Subjects can't be citizens, only ever slaves. Many Scots were and are socialists and internationalists, republicans and anti-imperialists. They don't hold with invading and occupying countries; theirs is a spirit of radical resistance and international solidarity. Seventy-five years down the line that same fighting spirit, that same rage against injustice, and that same hope for a better future persists. In Barcelona in October 2008, at an event to commemorate those who fought fascism, Willy Maley met the sons and daughters, nieces and nephews and grandchildren, of men and women who had served and suffered alongside James Maley in Spain. James never regretted going to Spain, and remained resolute in his passionate support for anti-fascist, anti-imperialist struggles around the world.

Although not an official war memorial – thanks to Britain's shameful policy of non-intervention – the statue of La Pasionaria on the Clydeside has since 2004 been a 'B' listed monument according to Historic Scotland. It was commissioned in 1974 by the International Brigade Association and unveiled on 5th December 1979. The sculptor, Arthur Dooley, was, like James Maley, and like the subject of his Glasgow commission, a communist.

Like the statue of La Pasionaria, From The Calton To Catalonia seeks to pay homage to a stirring and unprecedented episode in twentieth century activism and to celebrate the courage and internationalism of the ordinary men and women who played such an inspirational part in the struggle against fascism. The play was first performed at the Lithgow Theatre in the Pearce Institute, Govan, from 3-7 December 1990 as part of Glasgow's year as European City of Culture. We were extremely lucky in securing the services of Alex McSherry as director. The original cast included Gary Lewis and Libby McArthur, now stalwarts of the Scottish acting scene. The Lithgow was a small theatre seating around 120. The place was full for the last three nights of the five-night run. On the last night, Friday 7th December, James Maley and three fellow members of the International Brigades sat in the front row as guests of honour. They have all passed into history now. There have been subsequent productions, including a terrific performance by Greenock Youth Theatre Company

Kayos at the Tramway in 2004, and Basement Theatre Company back at the Pearce Institute again in 2011. The play has never been professionally produced but its early performances at Mayfest in 1991 and the Edinburgh Fringe in 1992, as well as the more recent productions by Kayos and Basement, were blessed by excellent performances, fantastic audiences, and favourable reviews. At a time when Scotland stands accused of being parochial and self-serving it is worth remembering that even in the throes of another time of austerity, Scotland was outward looking, passionately curious about what was going on in other parts of the world, and keen to play its part in the struggles for democracy and justice. We are grateful to Calton Books for reprinting the play and putting it back into circulation. Hopefully new readers will lead to further productions and help sustain the long-standing interest in Spain as part of Glasgow's radical history and legacy.

John Maley
Willy Maley
April 2014

James Maley with cast members of From the Calton to Catalonia, December 1990

Calton Books is a not-for profit INDEPENDENT radical bookshop established in Glasgow in June 2012 with premises at The Barras in the district of the Calton.

Why Calton Books?
This is but one story from Glasgow's proud working class history, sadly not many people are aware of it. We don't see any statues in George Square to these brave men or the countless other's - men and women - who have struggled for what they believe is right.

Sadly six weaver's lost their lives in their fight to defend their wages having been shot by the Militia on 3rd September 1787 near to were the Wellpark Brewery is situated today. Three died instantly, while three other's died over the next few days. Scores of other's were wounded but survived amongst the strikers were men, women and children.

Before the dead strikers were cold in their graves, the magistrates of the city agreed to reward the troops who had taken part in the action with a pair of stockings and a pair of shoes each. Colonel Kellet and the honourable Major Vere Paulet were awarded the Freedom of the city, while the other \officers were treated to dinner in the Tontine Tavern.

It is our undertsanding that the Calton Weavers had a Calton Book Club, we thought it would therefore be a fitting tribute to those who gave their lives in defence of working people's rights to name our shop - Calton Books.

We chose the name Calton Books in recognition of the fact that historically the first recorded strike in Glasgow was in 1787 undertaken by the weavers from the Calton.

We hope you agree that it is important to remember our history, to learn from the struggle of past generations and keep that memory alive as the working people's of this country continue to fight for the right to exist!

It is fitting therefore that the first publication being printed is **From the Calton To Catalonia** a play celebrating the life of Jimmy Maley from the Calton who seeing the plight of the Spanish people went to Spain to fight the fascist forces who were attacking the Spanish Republic.

Jimmy was one amongst many brave men and women from across the globe some of whom paid the ultimate sacrifice in what has been described as the prelude to the Second World War.

We are extremly grateful to Willy and John Malley for their permission to re-print their book and appreciate there help in facilitating this reproduction.

1st May 2014

Foreword

BILL ALEXANDER
Honorary Secretary, International Brigade Association.

"Picture it. The Calton. Fair Fortnight, 1937. Full of Eastern promise. Wimmin windaehingin. Weans greetin for pokey hats. Grown men, well intae their hungry thirties, slouchin at coarners, skint as a bairn's knees." A short time later in a prison, Salamanca, Spain. "They can dae whit the fuck they like. There's a war oan. Mind what happened tae yer man there. This is a prison, wee man, no a playhoose...... They lice oan ye son. Apart fae having absolutely nae sense a smell, they like tae coory intae the seams a yer troosers."

These were the experiences of James Maley and others from the Calton and Glasgow in the British Battalion of the International Brigade in Spain in 1937. Writers, dramatists and artists who illuminate history and bring to life the actions and ideas of the people fulfil their true responsibility, speaking for those who have no voice.

John and Willy Maley have fulfilled this in *From The Calton To Catalonia*, based on the true story of their father, James Maley. They have brought to modern life in a lively, enjoyable, popular form the story of a significant period of the past - the story of the International Brigade and the war in Spain.

Ralph Fox, an International Brigader killed in Spain, wrote "our fate as a people is being decided today. It is our fortune to have been born at one of those moments in history which demand from each one of us as an individual that he make his private decision...he cannot stand aside." What were the forces which led James Maley and his Glasgow comrades, sixty-five of whom were killed, not to stand aside but to leave their families and homes to fight in a distant land, Spain?

Life in the Thirties was hard: widespread poverty and want, unemployment bringing hardship and undermining personal pride. But in the streets people resisted despair by humour, fun and simple pleasures. There was help to neighbours and the less fortunate. Above all there was solidarity in resistance and struggle - stopping rent evictions, Hunger Marches to Assistance offices, even to London, demanding work and better benefits.

This solidarity stretched beyond the family, the street, the country to other lands and people. Fascism was then advancing over Europe. Its evil philosophy said that some people and races were superior and entitled to use force and terror against inferior races. It preached that war brought out the finest qualities in mankind. Amid their own problems the people of the Calton, and indeed all over the world, were angered by the treatment of the ordinary people in Germany and Italy by the fascist dictators. They understood that their own freedoms, limited though they were, were menaced.

When in 1936 the Spanish people fought back against the rebellion by Franco, aided by Hitler and Mussolini, the Calton recognised this kindred spirit and gave all possible help. Tins of food were collected door to door from meagre larders, pennies for bandages and medical supplies. The younger and some older, fit men volunteered to fight in the International Brigade alongside the Spanish fighters.

All help and aid demanded sacrifice and conviction. But the move from city life and then within a few days to be in actual battle made a supreme demand on the volunteers. They went to a strange country, eating unusual food, living and sleeping in the open, little time for training and learning the art of war, unable to practise with weapons because the British Conservative Government would not allow the Republic to buy arms. Fortitude, conviction and understanding of the highest order were needed to face the problems and build a military force.

There was no time! Franco's forces had failed to capture the capital Madrid by direct assault, stopped by the heroism of its inhabitants. He then attempted to cut the Madrid-Valencia road cutting off the capital from the rest of Spain. He attacked with his best, battle hardened professional troops helped by Hitler's Nazi machine gunners, tanks and planes. On February 12th 1937 the XVth International Brigade with James Maley and his Glasgow mates in the 600 strong British Battalion, few of whom had fired a weapon in anger, faced the overwhelming might of the fascist force. An advance of another half mile would have given Franco victory, the end of People's Spain and yet another country under the fascist heel.

The battle was fierce and bloody. In four days fighting 400 men of the

Battalion were killed, wounded or taken prisoner. In all 150 were killed on the Jarama front. The slogan "NO PASARAN" - "They shall not pass" became a reality. Franco never cut the road. Alex McDade from Glasgow, later killed at Brunete, expressed the spirit and pride of this first major trial in the song "The Valley Of Jarama" sung all over Spain and now at every International Brigade meeting.

The battle moved around the olive groves and hills and at times, with advances and retreats, the positions were confused. James Maley and thirty members of the Machine Gun Company were taken prisoner by the fascists. Three were shot in cold blood and the others lined up for execution. But the group was taken to the rear and imprisoned in the harsh conditions so vividly portrayed in the play.

They were brought to trial before a military court in Salamanca and charged with aiding a military rebellion - against Franco! Five were sentenced to death, the others to twenty years imprisonment. The British Government did not concern itself with their fate. But Franco, described by one Conservative MP as "a gallant Christian gentleman", arranged a parade of the prisoners in preparation for an exchange for fascist officers held by the Republic. They were filmed for Movietone News. The Brigaders' families back home caught sight of their loved ones for the first time in months when the newsreel was shown in local cinemas.

Home at last the returned prisoners joined the campaign to Aid Spain while five returned to Spain to rejoin the British Battalion and fight on. Finally Franco, helped by his fascist friends, defeated the people. World War II, which the volunteers had tried to prevent, began five months later, bringing with it widespread death and destruction.

Is *From The Calton To Catalonia* a nostalgic tribute to brave but misguided men in a wasted effort? The answer is a firm "No!" The volunteers, the activity of the Aid Spain movement, deepened people's confidence in their own strength and led to a hatred and understanding of the menace of fascism.

The lessons of Spain, the need for unity and struggle, influenced victory in the World War. The spirit of the Jarama slogan "NO PASARAN!" inspired the fighters at Stalingrad and Normandy, the firefighters in the Clydebank Blitz, the families on scant rations in the air raid shelters.

John and Willy Maley's lively drama portraying this spirit, helping the understanding of the past, has reinforced the activity of the people of the Calton towards the goal for all - A Good Life, Freedom and Peace.

Introduction

In the autumn of 1989, we were looking around for a suitable subject for a play for 1990, when Glasgow was to be European City of Culture. We ran over a list of events in Scottish history, searching for an image of Red Clydeside relevant to today - the Rent Strikes of 1915, the General Strike of 1926, the Hunger Marches of the Thirties. We finally settled on a story which was both Glaswegian and European. Based loosely on the experiences of our father, James, *From the Calton to Catalonia* is a prison drama set during the Spanish Civil War.

James Maley was taken prisoner at Jarama in February 1937, and endured five months in captivity. Unbeknown to James, his mother, then living in Shettleston, had spotted him in a Movietone newsreel in a local cinema. She pursued the reel to a picture house in Paisley and persuaded the projectionist to cut a couple of frames from the reel. This event inspired the play.

Directed by Alex McSherry, *From the Calton to Catalonia* was first performed in December 1990 in the Lithgow Theatre, Govan, with the following cast:

Mary Collins	-	Vicky Clarke
Jamie Collins	-	Colin Vetters
Ann Collins	-	Libby McArthur
Janet Cairns	-	"
Eddy Dixon	-	Mark Price
Lorraine Dixon	-	Ann Tierney
La Pasionara	-	"
Billy Cairns	-	Gary Stevenson
Mr Thomson	-	Gary Hagen
Glasgow priests	-	"
Daily Worker	-	"
Spanish officer	-	Chris McGowan
Spanish guard	-	Murray Campbell
Spanish prisoner	-	Dave Finlayson
Spanish priest	-	"

It was revived for a tour of community venues at Mayfest 1991, and again at the Arches Theatre in Glasgow for Trade Union Week in November 1991, when it was directed by Libby McArthur. Its most recent production was at the Edinburgh Fringe in 1992, where it was staged to critical acclaim by West Theatre Company, under the direction of Andrew Miller.

The authors would like to thank Gary Stevenson in particular for advice, support and criticism in the early stages of the play's initial production.

The authors wish to dedicate this play to James Maley, working-class activist, communist, International Brigader, and Spanish POW, and to all Red Clydesiders, past and present.

Dramatis Personae

Janet Cairns
Billy Cairns, P.O.W., her husband
Mary Collins, an usherette
Ann Collins, her daughter
Jamie Collins, P.O.W., her son
Lorraine Dixon
Eddy Dixon, P.O.W., her brother
La Pasionaria
Mr Thomson, a projectionist
two Glasgow priests
a Glasgow worker
a Spanish guard
a Spanish officer
a Spanish priest
a Spanish prisoner

CHORUS: Picture it. The Calton. Fair Fortnight. 1937. Full of Eastern promise. Wimmen windaehingin. Weans greetin for pokey hats. Grown men, well intae their hungry thirties, slouchin at coarners, skint as a bairn's knees. The sweet smell of middens, full and flowing over in the sun. Quick! There's a scramble in Parnie Street! The wee yin there's away wae a hauf-croon.

Back closes runnin wae dug pee and East End young team runnin wae the San Toy, the Kent Star, the Sally Boys, the Black Star, the Calton Entry Mob, the Cheeky Forty, the Romeo Boys, the Antique Mob, and the Stickit Boys. Then there wiz the Communist Party. Red rags tae John Bull. But if things wur bad in the Calton they wur worse elsewhere. Franco in the middle. Mussolini oan the right-wing. Hitler waitin tae come oan. When they three goat thegither an came up against the Spanish workers, they didnae expect the Calton tae offer handers.

The heirs a John MacLean, clutchin a quire a Daily Workers, staunin oan boaxes at the Green, shakin thur fists at the crowds that gethered tae hear aboot the plight ae the Spanish Republic. Oot ae these getherins oan the Green came the heroes ae the International Brigade, formin the frontline against fascism.

The Blackshirts, the Brownshirts, the Blueshirts, fascists of every colour an country came up against the men an women ae no mean city, against grey simmets an bunnets an headscarfs, against troosers tied wae string an shoes that let the rain in, against guns that were auld enough tae remember Waterloo. Fae nae hair tae grey hair they answered the call. Many never came back. They wur internationalists. They wur Europeans. They wur Scots. Glasgow should be proud ae them!

Scene 1: Action Replay

Green's Cinema, Rutherglen Cross, and Salamanca P.O.W. Camp, July 1937.

[The left hand side of the stage is the darkened cinema. The right hand side is the prison cell. There is no clear dividing line, with the whitewashed prison wall acting as the screen, and the projector and torch often the only means of lighting it. The prison is slightly raised on a platform, like a stage upon a stage. It has four bunks, a few crates, a table, and a straw floor. There is a barred window on the far right, which provides another source of light. On the far left, Mary Collins, torch in hand, harangues an imaginary audience offstage. In the background we hear the shouts and screams of excited children].

MARY: Right. Come on noo. Take yer seats. If yer no fast, yer last. Listen bawjaws, you fling wan mer bit a oarange peel an ah'll squeeze you tae the pips squeak. Come on. "If it's Green's its good". Hey, heid-the-baw. Lea the actin tae the actors. How miny poackits hiv you goat? Less a that. You were warned already. Ye coulda hid somedy's eye oot there. Aye its good. It goat a big write up in the paper. Ah don't care if ye've sat oan something. Change yer seat ur yer troosers, son. Listen tae gallus Alice. Ah know your mother. She's probably too ugly tae remember me. Naw, ye cannae get a shot. Because it belangs tae the cinema an ah buy the batteries. Ah'd like tae see you look sexy in this overall. At least ah've goat aw ma ain teeth, an they'll be in your neck in a minute if ye don't button it. Hoi, gingernut! You light that up in here an ah'll gie ye a hose doon fae the nose doon. Well hit im back, then. Hard. Look where yer gaun, missus. Ah know ah've goat flat feet, bit don't take me fur a doormat. Three chairs fur the big yin. She's fadin away tae a gable end. Did you hiv that ticket in yer mooth? Don't come wide, ur ah'm liable tae come snide. Wan toot an yer oot, wee man. Shut up, greetin face. Hurry up, hen. Yer gonnae miss the start a the picture.

[The lights come up. A man runs on stage. He is wearing a dirty vest and baggy trousers, braces dangling by his sides, and has a pillbox army cap pushed back on his head. A shot rings out. He falls. A Spanish soldier approaches the body from stage right, prods at it with his rifle, mutters a few words in Spanish, and walks off. A peasant woman emerges from stage left, kneels over the body, and asks a question in Spanish. The man says "Jesus Christ. Help me. Ah'm dyin!". The woman shouts something in Spanish and runs off stage left. She returns moments later with a priest, who gives the last rites, in Latin, to the dying man. The priest and the peasant woman exit stage left. The lights come down. The man remains flat on his back, centre stage. Mary Collins enters stage left].

MARY: (Mumbling to herself) Ah want tae see that bit again.

[Torch in hand, flashing against the backdrop. She is checking that no-one has left anything behind, shining her light between rows of seats. Mr Thomson, the projectionist, appears, balding and bespectacled, buttoning his jacket and adjusting his hat].

MARY: Hey. Haud oan a wee minute. Where dae ye think you're gaun?

MR THOMSON: (Condescending) I'm going home, Mrs Collins. I believe they call it 'knocking-off time'?

MARY: Ah'll knoack yer heid aff yer shooderz.

MR THOMSON: Mary! You've been watching far too many gangster movies!

MARY: Come on. Ye says ye wid let me hiv another look at that newsreel. Ah telt ye ah saw ma boay oan that thing.

MR THOMSON: You mean you thought you saw him? They all looked the same to me. Young men in uniform. Hard to tell them apart.

MARY: Ah know ma Jamie like the back a ma haun. God knows he's hid it oaffen enough. Noo get back in there an pit that reel oan.

MR THOMSON: (Firmly) No!

MARY: Can ye no jist let me hiv a look through it maself, then?

MR THOMSON: Mrs Collins. The equipment in that office is exceptionally delicate. It requires a trained professional hand.

MARY: Ah jist want tae see ma Jamie. Listen. Leave me yer keys an ah'll jist hiv a wee shufty maself.

MR THOMSON: Look, woman. I didn't go to college to learn my craft just so that you could have a 'wee shufty'. You're not touching that projector. Not without my supervision. It's more than my job's worth. You don't know the first thing about cinematography. Why, if the manager thought for a minute that I was even so much as contemplating tampering with that machine in order to satisfy some wild fancy of yours, he'd turn the two of us out into the street.

MARY: (Stage whisper) He's no tae know. Jist keep it quiet, an let me see the thing wan mer time, eh? Please. Ah've no seen him since Christmas. Ah might never see him again.

MR THOMSON: (Relenting) Oh, if you insist. I'll run through it tomorrow afternoon.

MARY: If you're windin me up ah'll run through you the morra efternin.

MR THOMSON: Yes, well. If you'll excuse me I'll be off home. (He exits).

MARY: (To herself) Three month noo an no a peep oot him. He ayewiz wanted tae be oan the big screen. Ah'd swear blind it wiz him, so ah wid. (She exits).

[Lights out].

Scene 2: A Day at the Movies

P.O.W. Camp, Salamanca, July, 1937.

[The lights come on in stage right, and we see the prison cell in Salamanca, Spain. The 'dying' man is now lying spreadeagled in front of two men who are playing cards. All three are unshaven, with close-cropped hair and clothes stained with dirt and sweat].

JAMIE: (In the same position as before, sprawled centre-stage, calling out in pain) Ah'm dyin!

BILLY: (Tossing a card down, shouting across to Jamie) Gie us peace! There's a war oan!

EDDY: (Chipping in) You get a grip for God's sake, son! If yer gonnae die, dae it quietly, wae a wee bit a dignity, eh? There's people in here tryin tae concentrate!

JAMIE: Ah'm dyin!

EDDY: (Sitting up). Listen, son. Wur aw dyin! Ah've no slept fur three nights oan the trot cause ae you.

BILLY: (Getting to his feet). It's him that's been oan the trot. (To Jamie) Hey, heid-the-baw! Are you tryin tae gas us? Ah think they pit you in here jist tae keep us oot the picture.

JAMIE: (Forcing himself into a sitting position, picking up the cap which lies beside him and putting it on) See yous heartless buggers, some bloody comrades, so yous are. Let's hiv a wee bit a solidarity.

BILLY: Judgin by the nick a your troosers, boay, you could be daein wae a wee bit a solidarity!

JAMIE: They cramps are killin me.

EDDY: Ah think that's how they issued us wae these keechy coloured ankle-stranglers. Camouflage, innit?

JAMIE: Don't make me laugh. An cannae haud it in when ah laugh.

BILLY: We've aw been through it, son. It'll pass.

EDDY: He's right, Jamie.

JAMIE: (Struggling to his feet) Three days runnin, an still "No Pasaran!"

EDDY: The morra's yer big day, son, ah'm tellin ye. We've aw had it. An we've aw moved mountains at the end of it. Talkin aboot movin, whit wis aw that stramash yesterday, eh? Somedy says they wur shiftin us aw again. Ah hate a flittin. Ye aye leave somethin behind.

JAMIE: In ma condition that wid be a blessin! Ah'm dyin fur a move, an ah'd like tae leave ma behind behind. But they've moved us twice already.

EDDY: Ah heard the third yin wiz yer last.

JAMIE: That's whit ah heard.

EDDY: Wan bullet in the back ae the bunnet-holder an its "Goodbye Tootsie, Goodbye".

JAMIE: They winnae dae that. (To Billy) Wid they?

BILLY: They can dae whit the fuck they like. There's a war oan. (Nodding towards the fourth bunk) Mind whit happened tae yer man there. This is a prison, wee man, no a playhoose.

JAMIE: Did any a yous see 20,000 Years in Sing Sing wae Spencer Tracy?

BILLY: Naw. Ah saw it wae ma wife. Spencer Tracy wiz washin his hair that night. Couldnae dae a thing wae the sink.

JAMIE: Ah wiz jist gonnae say, it wiz aw aboot bein inside.

BILLY: It wiz a picture, boay. Wisen up. Hiv ye ever done time?

JAMIE: Naw. This is ma first time.

BILLY: Ye don't know yer born then. Ye think this is haurd? See me.

When ah wiz your age ah done six month in Duke Street fur exercising ma democratic right. Broke a sheriff oafficer's jaw wae it, so ah did. Took a Benny wae the guy. (He laughs, raises his fist). Ye cannae argue wae that, by the way. Some a they bastards wur worse than any fuckin fascist. It wiz guns we needit, then, by Christ...

EDDY: (Screwing his finger against his temple) See him. He's pure mental, by the way. He nearly hooked his commandin officer at Jarama.

BILLY: Ah shoulda gubbed him wan. That guy wisnae the clean tattie, near he wiz. Wan a they university types, ye know. Soldier-daft tae the shootin starts. Captain tae. Haun-picked. (Makes masturbating motions with his hand) So anyhow. Five in the moarnin, right? Wur aw lined up. This Captain wae the bool in his mooth shouts "Fix bayonets!" Ah thoat he says "Fix bunnets!" So ah'm staunin' there like that. (Mimes adjusting an imaginery bunnet). Ah thoat we wur aw gonnae get wur photies taen or somethin. The hing is, wance the real fightin startit, wance we wur getting shat oan fae aw sides, yon Captain, where wiz he? (He puts his hand to his forehead as though searching for the Captain). Taen a powder, din't he?

JAMIE: Whit dae ye mean, he taen a powder?

BILLY: My, you've led a sheltered life, boay. It means he shot the craw, he flew the coup, he skied the pitch.

JAMIE: Aw, ah see.

EDDY: Ah don't blame the guy. Two weeks in the Terris disnae preper ye fur this. Ye know, ah saw some poor bugger that had goat bayoneted at Jarama. Spewed ma ringer, so ah did. Gie me the willies, they bayonets. See bayonets? Ye can stick them up yer arse!

JAMIE: Bayonets by Christ! Ah sat up hauf the night pittin a shine oan they things fur the whole bloody company. Couldnae sleep. Dead fidgety, so ah wiz. Wantit somethin tae dae wae ma hauns. Then the sergeant tells me ah had tae dirty it again in case it flashed in the dark an' gied oor position away! Ah'm tellin ye, ah coulda blinded the enemy wae the shine oan ma bayonet! Effin blinded them!

BILLY: You stoap effin an blindin, you.

EDDY: Shine up yer bayonet wae Brasso. Its only a tanner a tin. Ye get it oot Woolworth's fur nothin. Provided there's naebody in!

JAMIE: Did any a yous see A Farewell to Arms? Make an arse weep, so it wid.

BILLY: Furget films, you! Hiv ye read Marx?

JAMIE: Aye. Aw doon the backs a ma legs. Bloody beasties!

BILLY: No they kinna marks!

[The three men go into a Marx Brothers routine].

EDDY: (As Chico) I'm a gonna go for a sleep.

JAMIE: (As Groucho) Siesta?

EDDY: (As Chico) No, but I saw her sister. She sends her love.

JAMIE: (As Groucho) What about the five dollahs she owes me?

EDDY: (As Chico) You're a too old to be playin with dollahs!

BILLY: (As Harpo, has wrapped a sheet round himself, and produces a car horn) Toot! Toot!

JAMIE: (As Groucho) Oh, oh! Guess who's feeling horny?

EDDY: (As Chico) Ya goin a da party?

JAMIE: (As Groucho) I wouldn't belong to any party that would have me as a member. Besides, I don't like the Sanity Clause.

EDDY: (As Chico) That's crazy! Everybody knows there ain't no Sanity Clause!

JAMIE: (As Groucho) Did you come through the Pyrenees?

EDDY: (As Chico) Yeah. Now I need a new pair a trousers.

BILLY: (As Harpo) Toot! Toot!

JAMIE: (As Groucho) The traffic in here is terrible.

EDDY: (As Chico) Wanna buy some cigars?

JAMIE: (As Groucho) How much?

EDDY: (As Chico) Gimme a dime.

JAMIE: (As Groucho, checking his watch) Half past four. I berra be off. Call me a cab.

EDDY: (As Chico) Okay. You're a cab.

BILLY: (As Harpo) Toot! Toot!

JAMIE: (As Groucho) That'll be my cab. (Tries to jump up on Billy, who shrugs him off. Jamie faces Eddy again) Hey, haven't I seen you some place before?

EDDY: (As Chico) I don't think so. I never been some place before. Maybe you saw my brother. He's been some place before.

JAMIE: (As Groucho) Have ya gorra Lucky Strike?

EDDY: (As Chico) No, but I gorra General Strike.

JAMIE: (As Groucho) So what do we do if all the generals go on strike?

EDDY: (As Chico) I dunno.

JAMIE: (As Groucho) Why don't we call a General Strike and ask him?

EDDY: (As Chico) I got an idea. You call a General Strike and I'll call a General Franco!

JAMIE: (As Groucho) My money's on a General Strike!

BILLY: (As Harpo) Toot! Toot!

JAMIE: (As Groucho) Would you answer that? If its my first wife, tell her I'm out. If its my second wife, ask her where she spent last night.

EDDY: (As Chico) You gorra second wife? That's bigamy!

JAMIE: (As Groucho) Course its big a me! Its big a me. Big a her. Big of all of us. You got somethin against bein big, shortie?

EDDY: (As Chico) No. Whadda ya think a Mussolini?

JAMIE: (As Groucho) I prefer Macaroni. He's the guy who gave us the radio. We had to give him it back, though. Couldn't keep up the payments. Do you follow me?

EDDY: (As Chico) Yeah.

JAMIE: (As Groucho) Well stop it, or I'll have you arrested.

BILLY: (As Billy) Wid you two gie it a bye?

JAMIE: (As Jamie) Did any a yous see The Charge of the Light Brigade wae Erroll Flynn?

BILLY: (Menacing) Aye, ah saw it. Aw aboot the glory a the Empire.

Anti-Soviet propaganda intae the bargain. Whit aboot it?

JAMIE: Nothin. Ah jist liked Erroll Flynn's hair in it, that's aw.

EDDY: How come you're aye oan aboot movies?

JAMIE: Ma maw works in the pictures.

BILLY: Is she an actress?

JAMIE: Naw. She's an usherette.

EDDY: Whereaboots?

JAMIE: In the picture hoose!

EDDY: Whit wan?

JAMIE: Green's. At Rutherglen Cross.

EDDY: Really? Ah wiz broat up jist roon the coarner fae Green's. "If its Green's its good". That's whit the sign says.

BILLY: Ah wish tae Christ you two wid haud yer wheesht ur talk sense.

JAMIE: (Moves to the window) There must be a way oot a here.

BILLY: Aye, there is. Ye can get carted oot in a bag. Like yer man there in the coarner (Nods in direction of an empty bunk and a bundle of clothes). Nae skin aff ma nose, right enough. Ah'll hiv yer smokes.

EDDY: That's right, Houdini. The only thing that's gettin oot a here is the air that's escapin fae your troosers.

JAMIE: Some comrades! Yous might be content tae lie here an wallow in yer ain filth. No me!

EDDY: Look, if ye want ower the wall ah'm wullin tae gie ye a punt up. Ah could live withoot yer company an die happy.

JAMIE: (He seems to have finally found his bearings) Right! Ah've worked it oot. This is north.

BILLY: Yesterday it wiz west. Has the earth moved since then?

EDDY: Naw, but his bowels hiv.

JAMIE: Look! Its definite this time. That's north. Ah can see the North Star.

BILLY: Listen Galileo. The only stars you know aboot are in Hollywood, so don't act it.

JAMIE: (Changing the subject, claws at his legs) They lice are gien me gyp.

BILLY: (To Jamie) Take yer troosers aff.

JAMIE: Eh? Whit?

BILLY: Ah said gie us yer troosers aff.

EDDY: (To Jamie) Ah think he's missin his wife.

JAMIE: He'll be missin his heid in a minute.

BILLY: (Cigarette in one hand, holding out the other) Don't threaten me junior. (To Eddy) Get us a connel, bawjaws.

EDDY: (Saluting) Yes Sir! (Gets a candle).

JAMIE: (Backing away) You two turkeys hiv been cooped up here too long.

BILLY: (To Jamie) Cut the cackle an gie us they keech-catchers aff tae a delouse ye.

EDDY: (Handing Billy a candle) Here, don't waste it.

BILLY: (Lighting it with the cigarette) Listen, son. See this (Holding up the candle) This is the answer tae an itchy bum, an the solution tae scabby legs.

JAMIE: (Doubtful) Zat right? Tell me aboot it.

EDDY: He's tryin tae help ye son.

BILLY: They lice oan ye, son. Apart fae hivin absolutely nae sense a smell, they like tae coory intae the seams a yer troosers. Water'll no shift thum. Fire's the thing. Up an doon the seams wae a connel. That diz the trick.

JAMIE: (Coming forward with hand outstretched) Gie me it here, then. Ah'll dae it masel.

BILLY: (Handing him the candle) Go ahead, son. But ah'm an expert. Never burnt a per a troosers yet.

JAMIE: (Sits down on his bunk and starts running the candle down the inside of his trouser leg. A plume of smoke rises from his leg) Ayah bassa!

EDDY: Ah didnae know ye spoke Spanish, Jamie-boy.

BILLY: Hey, cloth-ears! Dae ye no think it wid be a wee bit easier wae them aff?

JAMIE: (Putting the candle out) Ah'll dae it efter!

BILLY: Whit is it, son? Whit's wrang? Are ye feart ye put us tae shame? Are ye hung like a hoarse, or whit? Jesus! Ye come ower a thousand miles tae fight fascism. Ye see yer comrades cut doon like dugs aw roon aboot ye. Ye get stuck in a shitehole like this in the middle a naewhere. An tae cap it aw, there's a guy here that thinks the sight a his wee man's gonnae send us intae shock. Come on, son. Wake up.

JAMIE: (Angrily, stabbing a finger at Billy) Awz ah wants ma privacy!

EDDY: Ye cannae hiv privacy in a prison, Jamie.

BILLY: Ats right, son. Ye cannae even get peace tae pull yersel.

JAMIE: Lea us alane!

EDDY: (Trying to head off a confrontation) We've seen ye in yer long johns already, Jamie. Its nae big deal.

BILLY: That's right. Yer vernear a grown man, fur God's sake!

JAMIE: Look, ah'm no wearin any underwer, right. Noo lay aff me!

BILLY: Yer no wearin anythin under yer troosers? By Christ, son, yer a true Scotsman, eh? Nae wunner yer bum's itchin! That cloth'll cut the baws aff ye!

EDDY: Yer underwear's aw that comes between you an armageddon, Jamie. Its yer last line a defence. A man's best friend is his drawers.

BILLY: Whit did ye dae wae yer long johns?

JAMIE: Ah flung them oot the windae!

EDDY: Whit made ye dae that?

JAMIE: Ah used them last night. Ah wiz dyin.

BILLY: (Collapsing and shaking with laughter) Haud me up Eddy. Dae you believe this guy? Jeez oh! Its a wunner they didnae jump oot the windae! Can ye know jist whistle oan them an they'll come runnin back tae ye?

EDDY: (Beginning to side with Jamie) Lea him alane, Billy. Lea the boay his dignity.

BILLY: Dignity? Don't talk tae me aboot dignity!

JAMIE: (To Billy) Whit dae you use, big man?

BILLY: Whit dae ye mean, "Whit dae ah use"?

JAMIE: Whit dae ye wipe yer erse wae?

BILLY: Ah'll wipe ma erse wae you if ye don't button it!

EDDY: (To Jamie) He wipes his erse wae his braces.

BILLY: Aw its like that, is it? Fly arse an shy arse gangin up oan me, eh? Ah'm well wide tae the two a yez. Look. (He goes over to the fourth bunk). Here. There must me somethin here ye can put oan. Stick yer man's breeks oan wance ah've burnt the beasties oot them, eh?

EDDY: Aye, Jamie. There ye are. If they're too long oan the leg ye can turn them up.

JAMIE: Whit dae ye think ah am, a graverobber? Ah'm no wearin a deid man's claes. No way.

EDDY: Whit's the problem? Ah've goat his socks oan. Whit good are they tae him?

BILLY: Nae good. Look. Ah'm wearin his vest. Long sleeves, man. Its bloody cauld in here at nights, you know that yersel. An check these oot. (Lifts one of his legs for Jamie to inspect his boots) These urnae parish boots, by the way. Feel that.

JAMIE: Naw thanks.

BILLY: (Putting his foot back down) That's beautiful leather. Soft as shite. Ah've jist no hid a chance tae dub them up right in here.

JAMIE: You two are worse than Burke an Hare, so yez are.

EDDY: Come on, Jamie. Be reasonable. Dae ye think the guy wid want us arguing ower his stuff, or pittin it tae good use? Fae each accordin tae his abilities, tae each accordin tae his needs.

BILLY: Exactly. This isnae wan a yer movies, boay. There's a war oan. Get doon aff yer high hoarse an take a look at the real world.

JAMIE: Hiv you guys nae respect fur the dead? It's no a bloody jumble sale. Fightin ower the guy's claes.

BILLY: Who's fightin? Noo whit ah'm ah bid fur these fine gentleman's troosers? Ma auntie's got a stall in Paddy's Market. She could sell rosary beads tae an Orangeman.

JAMIE: Could she sell Scotland doon the river?

BILLY: Sure! That's been done already!

[Jamie's mother enters stage left, torch in hand].

MARY: Shoosh doon there! There's people tryin tae watch the picture in peace! Come on, noo. Yous hiv sat through this twice already! Gie sumdy else a look in! Stoap crunchin lik that! This is a talkie, ye know! Ah'll hiv yez flung oot, the lot a yez!

[Music. Lights out. When they come back on, the men are in soft hats, double breasted suits, overcoats carrying violin cases. They do an exaggerated walk round, casing the joint].

BILLY: Okay you guys. Listen up. Here's the lowdown. That no-good bum Franco is tryin to grab a piece a the action.

EDDY: Yeah. An he's got that Nazi patsy Hitler to help him out.

JAMIE: An snub-nose Mussolini musclin in for what's left.

BILLY: So whaddaya say, guys? Are we gonna let those low-life schmucks kick the little guy in the teeth, or are we gonna make em eat lead?

EDDY: I say we hit em. Right between the eyes.

BILLY: Yeah. Then take them for a dip in concrete jackboots. (Wheeling round suddenly) Well, whadayaknow? A fascist. An we let im walk right in here! We gorra welcome committee, ain't we boys?

EDDY: Sure thing, boss.

JAMIE: You dirty fascist. You killed ma brother.

EDDY: Look at me ma. Ah'm on top a the world!

JAMIE: Need a little air in there?

[They open the cases, take out machine guns, and blast away. Lights out].

Scene 3: War Correspondent

Green's Picture House, Rutherglen Cross, December 1936; Salamanca P.O.W. Camp, July 1937.

[Stage left, Mary Collins, wearing overalls, sits at the back of Green's Cinema, just before Christmas, 1936. Off to the right, Billy and Eddy, in vests, are asleep in their bunks in Salamanca, seven months on. Jamie is propped up on one elbow reading a letter. His mother recites off to the left].

MARY: Dear Jamie,
 The New Year's drawin in an still nae sign a you comin hame. No sae much as a cheep oot ye. When yer bus left the Squerr last October ye says ye'd be back by Christmas. A lightenin war, ye says. Jist in an oot, ye says. Wee Ann has been frettin aboot ye. She's been sleepin in your bed. Ah call her Goldilocks. She's been readin oot tae me fae the papers aw aboot the war. Here ah am wringin ma hauns an wishin it wiz your neck.
 Ma legs is freezin sittin here, son. Ann taen ma bloomin stoackins away fur candy rock. Ah've been wearin your troosers in the scullery. Ye know how cauld it gets in there this time a year. Anyhow. Faither Kelly came tae the door the other day tae ask if there wiz any word fae Spain, an gied me a look that wid a turnt milk when he saw the state a me. "Ah'm the man a the hoose, noo", ah telt him. "Yer a mither way a duty tae yer daughter", he telt me.
 Ah think wee Ann's been kinna crabbit at school. Nae wunner. We've loast two men in as many years. We want you back in wan piece, son. Wae jam oan it. Mrs Cochrane came roon yesterday way a balaclava an a bag a soor plooms. Ah hope the balaclava comes in haundy. The wee yin ate the soor plooms. Yer a good boay, son. The whole street's been askin efter ye.
 Well, ah hope ye come back fae the front awright. Whit ah'm ah sayin? This is the front. It wiz you that deserted me, remember? Ah've pit a wee note in fae the wean. Ah think that's meant tae be a picture a you. No a bad likeness, eh? You look efter yersel, Jamie boay. Yer mammy loves ye. Wee Ann sends her smile.

[Jamie folds the letter, puts it in his breast pocket, takes out his diary, tears off a sheet, and starts scribbling. His mother holds the torch steady for him to see].

JAMIE: Dear Mammy,
 Ah goat yer letter awright. Ah kept meanin tae write. Ah've been keepin a diary. Ah know wee Ann'll want tae know aw the ins an oots a the war. Ah've been savin wee things fur her. They've goat stuff here

cawd marzipan. Sweet as hell. Wee Ann wid love it. Ah'll bring some back. Ah know a few words in Spanish. Jist enough tae get by. Ah don't think they're the sort a things ye wid learn at school. Ah'm keepin fine. (To give the lie to what he's writing, he goes into a violent coughing fit).
  Its a wee world, ma. Ah've met quite a few lads ower here fae Glesca, so its lik a hame fae hame. We hid a wee fitba team gaun fur a while. Then we loast the goalie. We're no aw angels wae dirty faces, maw. There's guys here that are oan the run fae aw kinds a bother - bad debt, the busies, broken merriages, haurd times at hame. There's quite a few unmerried faithers here. Ah've seen things that ah couldnae tell ye aboot. That's wan reason ah've taen sae long tae write.
  Ah feel closer tae ma daddy noo than ah did when he wiz alive. Ah miss ye maw. Tell Ann she can haud oan tae ma bed fur another wee while yet. That should keep her happy. Ah'll hiv presents fur ye baith when ah come hame. Aw ma love, Jamie.

[Jamie folds the letter, pockets it, and lies back on his bunk. The torch goes out].

Scene 4: The Messages

The Calton and Salamanca, July 1937.

[The Cairns house in the Calton. Janet Cairns is rocking a cradle where her baby sleeps. Billy sits on his bunk in Salamanca, cleaning his boots. Janet speaks to the baby. Billy addresses the audience].

JANET: Yer a good wee baby so ye ur. Ah've been daein mer greetin than you these days. Up tae high doe worryin aboot that da ae yours. Ah wish ah could sleep as sound as you.

BILLY: Ah hope yer lookin efter yersel an that boay a mine, Janet. Ah know it's hard oan yer ain. Jist you an the wean. Bit don't ye wonder whit kinda world waits fur him?

JANET: If he wanted a fight why did he no jist join the Calton Tongs?

At least he'd be hame at nights, chibbed ur no. Sure, there's fights closer tae hame int there? A coupla they scunners up it the broo could dae wi a good doin, ah'm tellin ye. Ye'd think the money wiz comin oota their ain bloody poakits.

BILLY: It's only hope fur the future makes the present bearable. You know that.

JANET: Ah'm that skint if ah drapped ma purse it'd float. Whit diz he think ah'm livin oan? Ye cannae live oan dreams.

BILLY: Ah know whit ah'm daein is right, darlin. You an the wee man are the reason ah'm here.

JANET: See me. Ah wish ah'd merried a pacifist. Trust me tae lumber a guy who thinks he's Glesca's answer tae Lenin.

BILLY: That Pasionaria's some wummin, so she is. "It's better tae die oan yer feet than tae live furever oan yer knees."

JANET: He couldnae look me in the eye that day he wiz leavin. His eyes were gaun every road but me.

BILLY: Ah'm sorry we hid words the day ah left.

JANET: Words are cheap. Ah wish breid wiz hauf the price a words. Ah wish food an love wur as cheap. Oh aye, he's away ower there beatin his breist lik naebody's business. You Tarzan, me beelin.

BILLY: Ah hope yer no gallivantin wae thon freends a yours doon that Barraland.

JANET: Ah've a bloody battle oan ma hauns jist feedin this bairn. Me an the wean ur wheezin away in this room. You might be fightin fascists, bit ah'm hivin a runnin battle wae the Factor. He's lookin mer lik Franco by the minute. Swear tae God. The sheriff oafficers had auld Nan Duffy's things oot in the street afore emdy knew whit wiz happenin. Nan wiz too bloody proud tae let oan. We managed tae save some a her wee bits an pieces. The big stuff wiz aw away oan the cart.

BILLY: Ah nearly pit doon ma bags an said ah wid stay when ye gave me thon look that mornin. Gutted, so ah wis.

JANET: If things don't get any better this next couple a weeks ah'll need tae pit this ring intae the pawn shoap. Ah cannae afford tae be sentimental, no in ma position. Ah've goat the wee yin tae think ae. Ah've goat responsibilities. Fightin Franco, by Christ! Ye can fight me, ya big stumour.

BILLY: Gie the wean a cuddle fur me. Ah miss ye. Ah love ye.

JANET: Love disnae buy the messages ur pay the rent.

Scene 5: The Purloined Letter

Salamanca P.O.W. Camp, July 1937.

[Billy and Eddy are sitting crosslegged, embroiled in a game of five stones. Jamie is perched on an upturned crate with 'Seville' written across it, playing a mouth organ. He hums a few bars of the 'Internationale'].

EDDY: Christ, man. Nae wunner yer winnin. Ye've hauns lik plates a meat!

BILLY: Don't talk tae me aboot plates a meat. Ah could eat a hoarse, saddle an aw.

EDDY: Aye. If ah hid an egg, ah'd hiv ham an eggs fur breakfast, if ah hid some ham.

[Jamie is now humming 'I Belong to Glasgow'. Suddenly he gets up, goes over to his bunk, rummages around, then turns to his cellmates].

JAMIE: Right, where is it? (Billy and Eddy go on playing). Come oan you fuckin per a coffin dodgers, whit hiv ye done wae it?

BILLY: (Without looking up) Done wae whit?

JAMIE: Ma letter.

BILLY: Ah'm sayin nothin tae ah've seen ma lawyer.

EDDY: Ah'm his lawyer.

JAMIE: Ye'll be his pall-bearer if ah don't get ma letter.

BILLY: Oh dearie me. Ah'll bet you wur a right tomboy when ye wur younger, eh?

JAMIE: Don't start me.

BILLY: Ah'll finish ye in a minute. Efter this gemme.

JAMIE: Where is it?

BILLY: Ah've wiped ma erse way it. Any obs? Its no the end ae the world. There's a war oan.

EDDY: (Putting his stones down) It wiz me that taen it, Jamie. Ah've planked it. We wur baith sick a listenin tae it. We know it aff by heart.

JAMIE: Aw. So ye've goat a heart, hiv ye? Next thing ye'll be tellin me ye've goat brains tae.

BILLY: Gie fanny features the letter, Eddy. Ma heid's lik a fuckin toayshoap.

EDDY: Its in ma shirt poackit.

JAMIE: (Getting the letter from Eddy's shirt) Ah wish you two wid grow up ur blow up.

EDDY: Look who's talkin! Greetin fur his mammy!

BILLY: (Producing a photograph from his back pocket) While yer at it, junior, ah taen this photie oot fae unner yer mattress. Yer girlfriend, ah suppose? Faur too good-looking fur you, son. Besides, she's auld enough tae be your mother.

JAMIE: (Snatching the photograph) It is ma mother! Look, ye've goat it aw wrinkled.

EDDY: Ah'll bet her nose is wrinkled anyway, efter bein pasted tae his erse aw efternin. (Jamie is staring at the photograph) Aw, he wants his mammy!

BILLY: Ah want his mammy! (To Eddy) Hiv ye seen her? A right wee smasher!

JAMIE: Chuck that, you! Wid you like me tae talk aboot your maw lik that?

BILLY: (Emotionless, matter-of-fact) Ma maw's deid. T.B. Ah never knew her. Everybody says ah've goat her eyes. (He throws down his stones, stands up and walks to his bunk).

EDDY: (Awkwardly, to Jamie) Ah'm sorry we taen yer maw's letter aff ye, Jamie. Ah suppose yer lucky tae hiv goat a letter. Naebody's ever sent me a letter. No that there'd be any point. Ah couldnae make heid nor tail a it.

JAMIE: How no? Is yer eyes bad?

EDDY: (Embarrassed now, wishing he hadn't opened his mouth) Naw. Ma eyes are fine.

JAMIE: If its no yer eyes, whit is it?

EDDY: Ah jist cannae make the words oot.

JAMIE: Whit dae ye mean, ye cannae make them oot?

BILLY: (Turning to Jamie) Diz he hiv tae spell it oot? Whit is it wae you? Can ye no get the message?

JAMIE: Whit message?

BILLY: (Nodding towards Eddy) He cannae read!

JAMIE: (To Eddy) Ah'm sorry, Eddy. Ah didnae know.

EDDY: Whit's tae be sorry fur?

BILLY: (To Jamie) Listen wean-brain. He disnae want a written apology. Jist drap it.

JAMIE: (To Eddy) Bit is there no...Ah mean, ah could....gie ye a haun...

BILLY: ...Ah said drap it! The guy cannae read. End of story.

JAMIE: The guy's goat a problem.

BILLY: That's his problem. No yours.

JAMIE: Some socialist you ur.

BILLY: Wisen up, son. The guy disnae want a big thing made aboot it. (To Eddy) Dae you want a big thing made aboot it?

EDDY: Ah'm no stupit.

BILLY: Naebody says ye wur.

JAMIE: Dae ye want me tae teach ye tae read? Ah've goat aw the time in the world. Think aboot it.

BILLY: Furget it.

EDDY: (Almost to himself) Disnae mean ah'm stupit.

BILLY: Aw fur fuck's sake!

[Lights out].

Scene 6: Food for Spain.

The Calton, July 1937.

[Two women - Lorraine Dixon, Eddy's sister, and Janet Cairns, Billy's wife - are wheeling a pram through the streets of the Calton, collecting for the Spanish Republic].

JANET: (Pushing the pram, which is laden with tins and packets) Food for Spain! Help the Spanish people in their fight against fascism!

LORRAINE: (Holding up a placard saying 'Food for Spain'. She stops and puts it down) Jeez oh! Ma legs are loupin. How faur dae ye think we've walked?

JANET: (Putting the brake on the pram) Aw, hunnerz a miles. Ah'm pure sweatificated.

LORRAINE: An how ur we daen?

JANET: (Poking at the contents of the pram) No bad. There's jist aboot enough here fur ma Billy's breakfast.

LORRAINE: Oh, cling peaches. Haud me back, Senorita.

JANET: Hauns aff. Noo get back up that close.

LORRAINE: Wild horses widnae drag me up that close. Ah told ye there's a big dug up ther.

JANET: Thurz folk ower there fightin Franco an you're scerd ae a dug?

LORRAINE: Ye shoulda seen the size ae it. There wiz enough meat oan that dug tae feed the entire International Brigade.

JANET: Who can afford tae feed a big dug nooadays? It wiz probably a chihuahua.

LORRAINE: Naw, it wiz a dug... Ah'm tellin ye, Janet, ah'm no gaun back in there. No way. Ah'm aw fur gaun oan tae the nixt street.

JANET: Awright. Haud oan the noo tae ah gie ma feet a wee rest. Ah knew ah shouldnae huv worn ma good shoes.

LORRAINE: Good shoes? Yiv only goat wan pair a shoes wummin.

JANET: At least ah don't get ma shoes oot the middens in Kelvinside.

LORRAINE: Shoosh!

JANET: Food fur Spain!

LORRAINE: Nae word fae Billy?

JANET: Naw. Nothin noo since the New Year. He wiz never wan fur writin, though. Could talk the hind legs aff a donkey, but never pit pen tae paper fae the day ah met him. Went away that sudden.

LORRAINE: Ye musta been shattered.

JANET: Ah gied him a look that wid've melted toaffee. But ah knew he wiz gaun. That night it came ower the radio, ye know, aboot them wantin help an needin volunteers, ah jist looked at him an ah says "Yer gaun, in't ye?" He says nothin. Jist went oan eatin. But ah knew. Ah could see it in his eyes. He wiz always a man fur causes, ma Billy. Its your brother that surprised me. Ah never thoat ae Eddy as the fightin kind. Nae offence.

LORRAINE: He thought aboot it a lot afore he went. He thinks things through, diz Eddy. Disnae make an exhibition ae himsel.

JANET: Talkin aboot exhibitions, whit dae ye make ae aw that money thur pittin aside fur yon Empire Exhibition next year? Ah mean tae say. Ten million quid fur a bloody carnival.

LORRAINE: It's a dampt disgrace. Money doon the drain.

JANET: Thur gonnae haud it oot at Bellahouston Park.

LORRAINE: Cowards that they ur. They widnae dare come near the Green.

JANET: Naw. They'd get a warm reception at the Haugh, that's fur sure. Second City ae the Empire. That's a laugh. At oor expense.

LORRAINE: Eddy wis crackin up aboot it afore he went away, him an aw his pals in the ILP. He wis talkin aboot gettin a big campaign gaun against it. Nae wunner. The last thing we need is an exhibition. Thurz people cannae make ends meet.

JANET: Yer no kiddin. Ten million quid, an here's me strugglin tae get by oan ten bob a week.

LORRAINE: They say it's the brainchild ae some fat-cat industrialist. Sir James Lithgow.

JANET: Brainchild? His brains ur in his erse. It's no exhibitions we need, it's joabs an hooses.

LORRAINE: Aye, an a wee bit a dignity. Thurz nothin in it fur us. Ah'll bet thurz somethin in it fur yer man Lithgow.

JANET: Aw aye. Nae doubt he'll end up wae some buildin named efter him.

LORRAINE: Ah hope ye hear somethin fae Billy soon. Oor Eddy's no wan fur writin. No a cheep oot him. Ye know, it said in the papers that when the jerries an the tallies come in their bombers the sky's black wae them. Thank God they're no drappin bombs here, eh? We've enough trouble wae bills, withoot gettin hit wae bombs.

JANET: Whit aboot yon wee place they flattened?

LORRAINE: Guernica.

JANET: Aye, Guernica. A wee toon the size a Clydebank. Vernear wiped it aff the map. They people are cryin oot fur help, an oor government sittin oan their hauns.

LORRAINE: But Eddy's no. Ne'er is your Billy.

JANET: Ye know, sometimes ah caw him fur everythin, Lorraine. Skivin aff an leavin me in the lurch. Bit Jesus, when ah heard the news aboot Guernica ah melted so ah did. Food for Spain!

LORRAINE: Still fightin fit, eh Janet?

JANET: Yer talkin tae the wummin thit knoacked a copper's helmet oaff in 1926. The boattles wur flyin at Brigton Cross. Ah flew in way a left hook. Move ower Benny Lynch. Food for Spain!

LORRAINE: Jeez oh! They musta heard that in Barcelona.

JANET: Ah hope buggerlugs heard it. Ah'm tellin ye, Lorraine, when ah broke it tae ma maw that ah wiz gonnae merry a communist she says tae me, "It could be worse, hen. He could be a soldier!" Look at me noo. Ten bob a week fae the Party, tae.

LORRAINE: Lucky you! Ah take it yer savin up fur a Persian rug?

JANET: Ah'd raither hiv a flyin carpet. Wae wan a them ah could scoot ower tae Spain an see how ma Billy's daen.

LORRAINE: Missin him, ur ye?

JANET: Ah don't know. (Pause) He can be a right bad bastard, ma Billy. Murder polis wae a drink in him. He could start a fight in an empty hoose. Maist nights he comes in lik a bear wae a burnt arse, crackin up at the least wee thing. (Angry) Ah'll tell ye somethin fur nothin, though. He'll never lift his haun tae me again, except tae salute.

LORRAINE: You tell him... Right, is the wagon train ready tae roll?

JANET: Haud oan. You'll need tae take a turn it pushin this pram. It's that heavy noo if it crashed intae a tram the tram wid come aff worse.

LORRAINE: Ye cannae hiv me pushin the pram. A single lassie. Folk wid talk. Ah've ma reputation tae think ae.

JANET: Aye. Folk might think yiv gave birth tae three bags a flour an twinty odd tins a beans. Right. Take the helm. Ye can shoogle it an kid on its goat a wean in it.

LORRAINE: Ah'll shoogle you in a minute! (Reluctantly takes hold of the pram).

JANET: (Shouting) Food for Spain! (To Lorraine) Spain. It's that faur away.

[Lights out].

Scene 7: Political Football

Salamanca P.O.W. Camp, July 1937.

[Billy is giving a pep talk to Eddy and Jamie. They are sitting crosslegged on the floor, while he paces up and down, jamming his fist into his hand to emphasise the points he is making].

BILLY: If ye come here yiv goat tae take whit's comin tae ye. Ah want tae hear nae mair complaints fae the pair a ye.

EDDY: Yes, miss.

BILLY: Ah mean it. Naebody says this wiz gonnae be a holiday camp. Ah don't want any huffin an puffin aboot the Communist Party. Yer lik a couple a greetin faced weans.

JAMIE: Aw ah says wiz ma uniform wiz too big, ah goat hardly anythin tae eat, an ah goat led intae an ambush lik a lamb tae the slaughter. (With resentment) An ah wish ma mammy wiz gettin ten bob a week fae the Party!

BILLY: Big deal. Wiv aw goat tae make wur wee sacrifices. Marx wid be turnin in his grave at the pair a yiz. (Stabbing a finger at Jamie's chest, then at his own). Ye might hiv broke yer mammy's heart, son, bit yer no gonnae brek mine.

EDDY: Aw Jamie's tryin tae say is that he thoat things wid be a bit better organized.

BILLY: Aw aye. Smart uniforms. A historic victory. A medal as big as a fryin pan.

EDDY: Look, Billy. If Stalin had gied us guns that fired we might no be in this bloody mess.

BILLY: At least he gied us somethin. Whit did the British Government gie us?

EDDY: Ye don't expect anythin fae the British Government! Ye expect a bit a internationalism fae a so-called socialist country!

BILLY: Whit dae ye mean, 'so-called'?

JAMIE: (Half to himself) Aw naw. No again!

EDDY: Ye know whit ah mean. Shootin auld Bolsheviks. Hardly fuckin socialism, is it?

BILLY: Haud oan. The Soviet Union is daen its best tae supply us wae whit we need.

EDDY: Fuck off. Hitler's gien Franco the best a gear. The fuckin Luftwaffe's bombin fuck oot the Republic, an Stalin sends ower rifles that don't work. The fascist that taen ma gun aff me laughed an said he wiz gonnae pit it in a fuckin museum. Wur gettin fucked aw ways fae whit ah can see. That's why wur losin.

BILLY: Wait a minute. Who says wur losin?

EDDY: Come on tae fuck. Ye heard whit the guards said. It's aw ower bar the shoutin.

BILLY: Propaganda. Wan a war's deadliest weapons. Don't let they bastards demoralize ye. Ye cannae lose heart noo guys. Think a the Russian Revolution. Think a Marx. There's the man that worked it aw oot. Capitalism. The Class Struggle. Revolution. Sure it's worth baggy troosers innit? It's worth pittin up wae nits in yer hair an durty beds. They jailed John MacLean dint they? Hounded him tae the grave. Did he gie up? Never. (Steps up on crate) "No human being on the face of the earth, no government is going to take from me my right to speak, my right to protest against wrong, my right to do everything that is for the benefit of mankind. I am not here, then, as the accused; I am here as the accuser of Capitalism dripping with blood from head to foot." (Steps down) If they dragged me oot the morra an pit me in front ae the firin squad ah'd sing the Internationale an spit in their eyes. Ye know whit yer here fur. Jist don't let go ae it.

JAMIE: Ye remind me ae a manager ae a midget fitbaw team ah used tae play fur. Wan day we wur playin a team fae the Sou Side. They hudnae loast a gemme. So the manager gies us this big pep talk in the dressing room. Wavin his fist. Shoutin the odds. Go oot ther an hammer them boays. Go oot ther an hammer them.

EDDY: An did ye?

JAMIE: We goat beat seventeen wan. The manager wiz greetin.

BILLY: Nae wunner. Wae you in his team.

JAMIE: Ah scored the goal.

[Lights out].

Scene 8: Off the Wall #1

Shettleston, July 1937.

[Ann Collins is bouncing balls, red and black, against the gable end].

ANN: (Rythmically, jauntily, as though she were reciting a nursery rhyme) Marxism-Leninism. Marxism-Leninism. Marxism-Leninism. Marxism-Leninism. Marxism-Leninism. Marxism-Leninism. (She drops a ball). Fascism!

[She picks up the ball and runs offstage].
[Mary Collins appears, selling sweets].

MARY: Last shout at the sweetie tray. Toaffy caramels, dainties, soor plooms, sherbet, liquorice an pokey hats. Get yer candy balls here. You keep yer hauns tae yersel, pal, ur ah'll gie ye three rapid. Come on noo. If yer no quick, yer sick. Never mind pickin an choosin, ya wee fusspoat. The nixt picture starts in two minutes flat. Try oor special gobstoppers. Four fur a haepenny, five if ah'm in a good mood. Get yer sweetie cigarettes an kid on its yer auld man's Woodbine. Nae jumpin the queue, noo. Wan at a time, wan at a time! Make yer mind up, wull ye? Here, hiv ah no seen your face afore? Zat right? Well yer twin bought enough toaffy tae dae the two a yez. Ye'll soon hiv nae teeth left tae make a face lik that. You're needin a rub doon fae the gub doon. Hoi! Whit hiv ah telt you aboot flickin bogeys? Can ye no wipe them unner yer seat lik everybody else? Jesus Christ. Ah've goat a bloody stampede oan ma hauns an ah'm jist aboot cleared oot a everythin. Ah'll hiv tae heid them aff it the pass.

[Mary exits].

Scene 9: The Religious Divide #1

A Chapel in Glasgow's East End.

1st GLASGOW PRIEST: Many of you have asked about the attitude of the Church to the war in Spain. The Church does not have a political role to play in that tragic affair, but it does have a moral and spiritual duty to provide guidance to its members. And it is with this duty in mind that I am bound to say to you that we cannot but condemn, morally and spiritually, those anarchists and communists who burn churches, murder priests and nuns, and terrorise innocent communities. We cannot but condemn, morally and spiritually, those among us who have abandoned their families, their homes, their neighbours, and their responsibilities, in order to fight for an atheistic republic. They are not heroes. They are deserters. We cannot but condemn, morally and spiritually, those who wilfully seek to aid and abet, whether through propaganda or by violent means, the same unworthy cause. Let us pray.

[Jamie approaches the priest and kneels beside him. The priest blesses Jamie, and hands him two oranges which he produces from the pockets of his cassock].

Scene 10: Orange Order

The P.O.W. Camp in Salamanca, July 1937

[Jamie walks back to his cell and holds up the oranges to Billy and Eddy].

JAMIE: Look whit ah got fur ma second communion.

BILLY: Hey, where'd you get them?

JAMIE: The priest gave me them. Oan condition that ah renounced Marx as the Anti-Christ.

EDDY: Blood oranges.

BILLY: Gie me them ower. (Jamie tosses them over, one at a time. Billy catches them) Ah don't believe ma eyes. Did you steal these? Ye'll get us shot.

JAMIE: Ah told ye. They're a wee present. (Billy juggles with the oranges).

EDDY: Hey, that's no bad Billy.

BILLY: And now for my next trick. (He puts the oranges up his vest. Eddy wolf-whistles).

JAMIE: Stoap that you.

BILLY: Aw ah needs a wig an ah'll make ma escape.

JAMIE: Gie us them back.

BILLY: Feel ma tits furst.

JAMIE: Shut it.

EDDY: Go an see the governor. He'll mibbe repatriate ye.

BILLY: Repatriate me? He'll marry me. Heah Jamie. Watch ye don't trip ower yer bottom lip. Come ower here. Ah'll teach ye aw aboot the burds an the bees. (Recognizing Jamie's discontent) Better take these oot. Don't want tae get you guys too excited. Ah'll need an armed guard posted it ma bed the night. At least wiv got a baw noo. (He drops one of the oranges and dribbles with it. Eddy tackles him. Jamie huffily intervenes).

JAMIE: Gie us ma oranges back.

BILLY: Spoilsport.

EDDY: Oor baw's been requisitioned fur the front.

JAMIE: Uch, it's aw squashed noo. (He huddles up on his bunk).

EDDY: Jamie? Jamie? Eat wan a yer oranges. They're good fur ye.

BILLY: Ye'll no grow up big an strong if ye don't eat yer oranges. (He goes over beside Jamie's bunk. Knocks on the floor) Is Jamie in? (Knocks again) Is Jamie comin oot?

JAMIE: Naw.

BILLY: Well ur his oranges comin oot?

[Lights out].

Scene 11: Back Home

The Calton, July 1937.

[The kitchen in the Cairns's house in the Calton].

JANET: That's the wee yin doon fur the night.

LORRAINE: Ye'll be gled a that.

JANET: Yer no kiddin.

LORRAINE: Must be a haunful oan yer ain.

JANET: Uch, it wiz a haunful when Billy wiz here. He wiznae much ae a help tae me.

LORRAINE: Ye need a brek, hen. Ye need tae let yersel go.

JANET: Ah wish ah could let masel go. Ah'd let masel go right oot that door an no come back.

LORRAINE: Ye cannae dae that.

JANET: Ah know ah cannae. He could, bit ah cannae.

LORRAINE: Whit you need is a wee night oot. Let's you and me get oan wur glad rags an go up the Barraland this Seterday, eh? Yer maw'll watch the wean.

JANET: Naw she'll no. Oh, she'll watch him if ah'm oot collectin fur Spain, ur if ah'm runnin aboot lik a blue arsed-fly tryin tae tap enough tae get by oan, bit she'll no babysit fur me tae go oot an enjoy masel...

LORRAINE: Whit aboot ma maw? She'll take him fur a night.

JANET: Whit's the point? Ma maw wid get tae know an ah'd be made tae feel lik a scarlet wummin.

LORRAINE: Stoap feelin sorry fur yersel.

JANET: How? Ah'm sick fed up wae scrapin. Look at the state ae me. Ah'm an auld wummin afore ma time.

LORRAINE: Come oan, Janet. Yer ma best pal...an yer ain worst enemy. Sittin ther mopin.

JANET: Haud oan. Ma maw disnae want me tae go tae the dancin an you don't want me tae feel sorry fur masel? Ah've tae pit a brave face oan, is that it? Play the happy housewife? How can ye keep the home fires burnin when ye've no goat the money fur coal?

LORRAINE: Ye can try, Janet. Ye can light a connel...

JANET: It takes mer than a connel tae heat this bloody hoose. Ah'm no Joan of Arc. Ah'll bae naebody's martyr, Lorraine.

LORRAINE: Ah can unnerstaun ye bein bitter, bit whit aboot the sacrifices Billy's makin, eh? Dae ye think he's no sufferin? Jist haud yersel thegither tae he comes back.

JANET: Things wurnae sae great when he wiz here. Ah don't know whit he'll come back like, an ah don't know whit he'll come back tae.

LORRAINE: He'll come back tae you an the bairn, Janet. Things'll work oot.

JANET: Wull they? Ah'm no sae sure. When ma da came back fae the Great War ah didnae know him. Ah wiz jist a wee lassie. Ah wiz feart ae him. So wiz ma maw. He used tae sit an ster intae the fire, sayin "Aw the bonny kilties, dyin in the mud." It took a long time fur things tae settle doon in oor hoose. Ah used tae hear him greetin at night. Hated him fur it. Some childhood that wiz. Jumble sale claes an a da ah wiz scerred ae. Ah want ma weans tae fare better than that...Oh Lorraine, ah'm scerred! (They embrace).

[Lights out]

Scene 12: Boxing Clever

The P.O.W. Camp in Salamanca, July 1937.

[Billy and Eddy are playing cards on an upturned crate. Jamie is lying on his bunk reading].

BILLY: (Throwing down a card) Ah'm out! (Turning to Jamie) Hey, young yin! Are you in?

EDDY: If yer no in, ye'll no win!

JAMIE: (Shouting across to Eddy) Is that big yin no done cheatin ye?

BILLY: Ah'm beatin him ferr an squerr. Ah'm a pure shark at the gemme. Howzaboutit. Feelin lucky, son?

JAMIE: Naw.

BILLY: Come oan, you. Start gettin intae the social company an stoap lyin there givin yer privates the clenched fist salute. Ye'll go blind.

JAMIE: Ah'm readin.

BILLY: That's even worse fur yer eyes! (Shuffling the pack, smiling at Eddy, addressing Jamie) Tell me, son. Whit's a nice boay lik you daein in a place lik this?

JAMIE: Ah telt ye. Ah'm tryin tae read.

EDDY: Whit are ye readin? Its no that bloody letter again, is it?

JAMIE: Naw.

EDDY: Its no the Evenin Times by any chance, is it? Ah've no heard the results fur six month. The season's ower an ah've heard sweet F. A. since the New Year.

BILLY: Ah wunner how Celtic goat oan in the league?

EDDY: They'll hiv been oot thur bloody league. Jist lik us.

BILLY: Uch, away an shite in a bucket an rattle it. McGrory'll hiv been scelpin them in, ah'll bet. (Gets up and mimes a Celtic goal complete with commentary) Wilson to Crum. Back to Kennoway. To Scarfe. He's got Napier to his left. Still Scarfe. To Crum. The forward pass beautifully brought down by McStay. He's looking for McGrory now. Its a high curling ball, a header, and a goal. (The motions of the game have brought him over to Jamie's bunk) Whit aboot you, young yin? Ur ye intae the fitbaw, ur is netbaw mer your gemme?

JAMIE: Ah played furri school. Ah coulda goat a trial fur St Mirren.

BILLY: You couldnae get a trial fur Stalin.

EDDY: (Barging in) You get a fuckin grip! Is there anythin you'll no laugh at, ya mad bastard? Fuckin show trials, millions murdered, an you're gonnae make a joke oot it?

BILLY: (Taken aback. To Eddy) Haud oan. (Nodding towards Jamie) The guy's tryin tae tell me somethin. (To Jamie) Noo. Ye wur sayin aboot St Mirren?

JAMIE: (Excitedly) Aw aye. They sent a scout tae see me. Ah wiz built fur speed. Ah hid the pace a Patsy Gallacher an the strength a Alan Morton.

BILLY: (Flapping his arms) If ah hid the wings uv a sparra. If ah hid the arse uv a crow...

EDDY: (Butting in beside him)...Ah'd fly over Parkheid the morra, an shite on the bastards below.

BILLY: (Raging) Don't start me. Ya fuckin dunderheid. Ah wiz gonnae gie ye a couple a yer smokes back tae. No noo.

EDDY: Ah wiz thinkin a gien it up anyway.

BILLY: Whit? Smokin?

EDDY: Naw. Playin cards.

JAMIE: Look. If you two ur gonnae fight ah'm gaun back tae ma book.

BILLY: (To Eddy) Listen tae it! (Very polite) I'm going back to my book! (To Jamie) So whit's the book, son? Whit is it yer readin?

JAMIE: Its ma diary, if ye must know.

BILLY: Yer 'diary'? Thur better no be anythin aboot me in there, ur ah'll pit a fuckin match tae it.

JAMIE: Thur burnin books in Germany. Ye need tae keep a record a whit happens. Ye've goat tae write things doon. Ah want people tae know whit we went through, an why we done it.

BILLY: Its no books that'll beat fascism, it's bullets an bombs.

JAMIE: Ye need tae change the way folk think.

BILLY: Ats whit ah'm sayin. Blaw the shite oot them. Make them see sense.

JAMIE: (To Eddy, indicating Billy) Don't listen tae that big eejit. He's full a it.

BILLY: (Getting to his feet) Less a your lip, son, or ah'll fatten it fur ye.

JAMIE: You an yer fists. That's your solution tae everythin.

BILLY: If it's good enough fur the bosses, its good enough fur me.

JAMIE: There's other ways a changin things than violence.

BILLY: Don't go preachin yer pacifism tae me, ya wee baw-bag. You didnae come ower here fur the fresh err an sunshine, did ye? Look. Ye cannae fight fascism wae empty hauns. Ye cannae appease Nazism. Ye cannae beg the bosses fur a payrise. Ye need mer than a pen in yer fist tae change the world.

EDDY: (Butting in) They say the pen is mightier than the sword. Frankly, ah'd raither get chibbed wae a pen.

BILLY: When ah want contributions fae the fler ah'll ask fur them.

EDDY: There's goat tae be a wee bit a give an take, Billy.

BILLY: (Clenching his fist in front of his face) Gie them that an take whit ye need! Thats ma philosophy. Imagine a boot comin doon oan a face forever. That's the only way tae deal wae fascism. Grind it right doon intae the dirt. No mercy. No way, Jose. Spain is gonnae be fascism's funeral pyre. Ye've goat tae fight fire wae fire.

EDDY: Ah'd hiv thoat watter wiz a better bet.

BILLY: Force is the midwife of an auld society givin birth tae a new wan.

JAMIE: An ah suppose we're the midwives?

EDDY: Naw. We're the hoat watter an towels.

JAMIE: (Sniffing his armpits) Speakin a which, we could aw be daen wae some.

BILLY: Never mind. When ye get hame yer mammy can gie ye a sponge-doon in the sink. (Looking around) Here. Fancy a game a fitbaw?

EDDY: Whit wae?

JAMIE: (Nodding at Billy) His heid!

EDDY: Naw. Too hard. Ye need a baw wae a bit a bounce in it.

BILLY: (To Jamie) Whit aboot thon oaranges ye nicked?

EDDY: We ate them.

BILLY: See whit ah've goat tae pit up wae in here! (Looking for something else to occupy himself with) Right! (Grabs his mattress off his bunk and thrusts it at Eddy). Haud that up in front a ye.

EDDY: (Taking hold of the mattress) Whit fur?

JAMIE: He's makin a den.

BILLY: (To Jamie) You're no gettin in it. (To Eddy) Are ye haudin it tight, man?

EDDY: (Peering round) Whit are ye daein roon there?

BILLY: (Shadow boxing) Warmin up.

EDDY: (Looking back at Jamie) Has he pit a match tae it?

JAMIE: Ah think he fancies hissel as Benny Lynch. He's goat the gut fur it, right enough. The British bevvyweight champion. Ye better get doonwind ae his ringside.

BILLY: Bum away, son, yer bum's yer ain. Bit your oan next, mind.

JAMIE: (Sitting up) Any time. Ah did a wee bit a boxin efter ah left school.

BILLY: Whit it? Paperweight?

JAMIE: Naw, flyweight.

BILLY: Aye, yer a wee flyman, awright. Yer gonnae need a fuckin parachute if ah catch ye wae wan a ma famous jawbrekerz.

EDDY: When are ye gonnae hit me?

BILLY: (Starting to jab at the bedding) And the big southpaw hits him with a left, and a left again, and another left.

JAMIE: Ah think he favours his left. Ah could take him in three rounds.

BILLY: (Still jabbing away) Whit are you sayin? You couldnae go three rounds in the Sarry Heid.

EDDY: (Unsighted, commentates from behind the mattress) And Lynch now, taking the punishment, mopping it up, and asking for more. You just can't put this man doon. He's taking everything his opponent has to offer. He takes a left, a right, a centre. An uppercut. A rabbit punch. A jab. (To Jamie) Hiv ah missed anythin oot?

JAMIE: A knockout?

BILLY: Right! (He puts all his weight behind a last punch. Eddy disappears under the mattress and Billy lands on top of him).

JAMIE: Dae a count?

EDDY: (Strained) Ah think its a split decision.

BILLY: (Getting to his feet on top of the mattress and Eddy) And the winner is...

EDDY: (Rolling the mattress and Billy off him, and struggling to his feet) Fast Eddy fae the Gorbals!

BILLY: (Getting up) Bit haud oan a wee minute! The judges hiv reversed that decision. Battlin Billy fae the Calton is the new world champion. An the crowd go crazy. (He stands with one foot on the mattress, hands clasped above his head in triumph).

EDDY: (Placing a foot on the mattress) And its all over. Franco's down and out. The jawbone of his arse his been broken in two places.

JAMIE: (Joining in) And what a pathetic performance it was from the sparring Spaniard, General Francisco Franco y Bahamonde. He showed all the courage and control of a burst mattress there as the jawbreaker from the Calton went at it hammer and tongs.

BILLY: Fascism is on the ropes, and its all thanks to the Glasgow gobstopper. They'll be singing his praises now, from the Calton to Catalonia.

EDDY: Catalonia! Christ, Billy. We saw some sights comin through that place. Made me feel as if ah'd been turnt inside oot. (To Jamie) Aw the lines wur doon, but there wiz boadies strung oot alang the pylons. Wan poor bastard wiz starkers. Somedy hid taen his daddy's medals aff him.

JAMIE: That musta been they Moors. Ah heard they dock yer weddin tackle, that's whit ah heard.

EDDY: Ah heard that tae. Whip the Bolsheviks aff ye as soon as look at ye, that mob. Finish aff the wounded as well. Nae mercy, they Moors.

BILLY: (Angrily) That's aw jist propaganda! There's a war oan. Naebody's hauns is clean. There's blood oan every heid.

EDDY: Ah saw it wae ma ain eyes!

BILLY: Did ye see who done it?

EDDY: Naw.

BILLY: Then how dae ye know it wiz the Moors?

EDDY: Castration, man. That's their trademark, innit?

BILLY: Away ye go! (Turning to Jamie) Listen. When we set up wur furst camp, there wiz a boay hung. When ah saw him at first ah thoat some bugger hid set up a punchbag. Ah wiz gonnae go an hiv a wee workoot. Poor wee mite. Couldnae hiv been mer than twelve.

JAMIE: Mibbe he done hissel in?

BILLY: He'd hiv hid a joab tyin his ain hauns behind his back. Turnt oot he'd been caught stealin supplies.

EDDY: Fuck that fur a game a sojerz. Whit aboot thaim Gestapo. Ah heard they dae aw sorts a hings tae prisoners. Ah heard ye take death as an aspirin when they bastards ur finished wae ye.

JAMIE: "Man's inhumanity tae man..."

EDDY: "...makes countless thousands mourn."

BILLY: (To Jamie) Uch, whit dae you know? Diz your mammy know yer oot?

JAMIE: She disnae know if ah'm deid ur alive.

EDDY: Jist as well.

JAMIE: You two think ah know nothin, daen't ye?

BILLY: Next question.

JAMIE: Ye know, jist before ah goat taken, we wur croassin a field. Pitch black it wiz. We wur aw haudin oantae wan another. We gets haufway acroass when somedy starts shootin the shite oot us. We aw hits the dirt. Turns oot shots ur gettin fired fae this farmhoose. How the fuck they could see us ah don't know. They musta smelt us comin. Anyhow. A few ae us cut roon the back an flung in a couple a grenades.

Torched the place. When the smoke cleared we went in an found them. A boay an a lassie. They made an auld man a me. Weans wae guns. We blew them tae bits. 'No Pasaran' written aw ower the wall. Maw an da musta been aff fightin fur the Republic. They thoat we wur Franco's men.

BILLY: In a war it disnae matter whit size a shoe ye take. Ye get yer haun oan a gun, an yer arse is oot the windae.

EDDY: How come they stoapped the wummin fae cerryin guns? If ma sister wiz here she'd want a rifle in her hauns an a bandoleer ower her shooder.

BILLY: Aye. Look at La Pasionaria. In a real people's army wummen an men should staun shoulder tae shoulder.

JAMIE: If ye'd seen the boadies piled up against the barricades in Madrid ye widnae be sayin that.

BILLY: (Surprised) Haud oan. When wur you at Madrid?

JAMIE: Last year. Durin the siege. Wan big cemetery, so it wiz. Women aw ages. Aye, an wee lassies tae. Broke the men, so it did. Broke them. Nae wunner they stoapped them fae fightin at the front.

BILLY: Uch! A corpse is a corpse. Wance ye've seen wan ye've seen them aw! Worms cannae tell them apart. There's a war oan. Who can see straight? Who can think straight? Look whit happened the night we goat here. Bastards!

EDDY: Ah think ah'm gonnae be sick.

BILLY: (Pulling away his mattress) No oan ma bed, yer no.

JAMIE: (Gazing off into space, remembering, almost to himself) Aye. Madrid. (Pause. Billy and Eddy look at him with a mixture of admiration and surprise). See when we marched in tae the city. Thur wiz posters an banners an flags everywhere. Like coronation day, so it wiz. The whole toon came oot tae meet us. Cheerin an singin, so they wur. Hauf us hid oan Russian uniforms - no the full kit, jist a hat here, a jaicket there, the odd pair a troosers - an the Spaniards thoat the Russians hid come: "Salud! Salud!", they shoutit, "Salud! Salud! Han venido los Rusos!", "The Russians have come". Ah tried tae tell them ah wiz fae Shettleston, but wan fella telt me in English that he couldnae speak Russian, but he wiz glad we'd come. Ma wee squad endit up wae wan uniform atween six a us. Furst up wiz the best dressed. Mental, so it wiz.

EDDY: Whit Battalion wur ye wae, then?

JAMIE: Paris Commune. A right mixter maxter. Maistly French, as ye'd expect, bit a fair smatterin fae other countries. Ah cawd it the bunnet brigade. Fur some strange reason everybody seemed tae think a bunnet, a beret, ur a balaclava oaffered some protection against bullets an bombs. Oor lot hid wan tin hat between us an we used it as a poe.

EDDY: Dae ye speak French, then?

JAMIE: Naw, bit that didnae worry them. They didnae think ah spoke English either. They thoat ah wiz a Russian as well. Ah jist went alang wae it fur a laugh. They cawd me 'Son of Stalin'. (Billy laughs) Ah thoat that wid appeal tae you. Ah took it as an insult, bit ah couldnae complain. Ah goat the red carpet treatment aff them. Two month ah wiz there. Then we wur aw wheeched back tae Albacete fur another stint a trainin.

BILLY: Ye know son, it wiz the defence a Madrid that finally made up ma mind aboot gaun tae Spain. La Pasionaria. Her voice oan the radio. Made the hairs oan the back a ma neck staun tae attention, so it did.

EDDY: Me tae. When ah heard aw aboot the men an women at the barricades ah knew ah had tae help. An tae think that you were there, Jamie. You were there when history wiz bein made. Ah mean, ah thoat a masel as an activist, ye know, marches an that. (Holds his fist, clenched, in front of his face) Bit comin face tae face wae fascism. That's somethin else!

BILLY: (Looking Jamie up and down, still trying to take it in) Madrid by Christ! Imagine you bein there! At the siege!

JAMIE: (Warming to his subject now) It wiz lik wan big warrant sale, ah'm tellin ye. Aw the furniture wiz oot oan the streets. Some folk wur sittin oan rockin cherz behind the barricades. Makin music. Singin songs. (Turning up the table and standing behind it, mock rifle in hand). Then they came at us. 'No Pasaran!' The cry went up alang the lines a tables an chairs an chests a drawers. 'No Pasaran!', the shout rang roon the squerr an up the sidestreets. 'They shall not pass!'

EDDY: No Pasaran!

BILLY: No Pasaran!

[Eddy grabs the soup basin and starts beating it with a spoon. Billy plays the flute. 'Bandiera Rossa'].

Scene 13: Off the Wall #2

Shettleston, July 1937.

[Lights up. Ann Collins is once again bouncing her balls against the gable end between cinema and prison].

ANN: Class struggle, armed struggle. Class struggle, armed struggle. Class struggle, armed struggle. Class struggle, armed struggle. Class struggle, armed struggle (She drops a ball). Appeasement!

[She picks up the ball and runs offstage].

Scene 14: The Religious Divide #2

Another Chapel in the East End of Glasgow, July 1937.

[Lights up. A priest stands at a pulpit, bible in hand, and addresses the audience].

2nd GLASGOW PRIEST: I would like now to turn your thoughts to the civil war presently raging in Spain. Some of you here today have friends or relatives who have made the ultimate sacrifice, giving their lives in the cause of freedom and justice. Our hearts go out to you. I know there are those who say that it is not the business of the Church to become embroiled in political affairs. That view is not shared in this community. When a people are at war with a tyrant, one cannot do as Pilate did, and wash one's hands of all social responsibility. The Church has a mission, and that mission is the defence of Christian values, values which, in Spain, are threatened by the spectre of fascism. There is a plate going round at this moment, and I would ask you to make whatever contribution you can, however small. Fascism is an evil that has to be faced up to and fought against. That fight costs money. It also costs lives. Let us do what little we can to help.

[He blesses himself, bows his head, and walks off. Lights out].

Scene 15: The Dream

Salamanca, April and June 1937.

[The dead of night. The men are all in bed. The fourth bunk is occupied. Billy is talking in his sleep. He moans, then starts shouting].

BILLY: Mucho malo! Mucho malo! Bastards! Bastards!

[Billy is dreaming about an event that happened three months earlier, the night the men were moved to Salamanca. Suddenly the door bursts open. Two guards and an officer enter. Billy is transfixed].

1st GUARD: Rojos conos!

2nd GUARD: Todos los extranjeros, aqui!

OFFICER: (Dragging the fourth man from his bunk. He is obviously sick and has trouble standing up. The officer puts a pistol to the prisoner's head) Hay que tomar la muerte como so fuera aspirina.... Espana?

GUARDS: Uno!

OFFICER: Espana!

GUARDS: Grande!

OFFICER: (Cocking the pistol and taking hold of the fourth man's arm) Espana! (At this point in the Nationalist litany, Billy shouts along with the guards).

ALL: Libre!.

[The officer pulls the trigger and the fourth man's head jolts, but he does not fall as he is being held. Billy moves forward, but is forced back by the guards at gunpoint. The officer lets the body drop. He points his pistol at Billy and gestures toward his bunk. The guards shoulder their rifles, take the fourth man by the legs, and drag his corpse out. The officer leaves last, walking backwards, spitting as he exits. The door slams. Billy starts shouting again].

BILLY: Bastards! Bastards! (Jamie and Eddy wake up, get out of bed, and shake him).

EDDY: Whit is it, man? Whit's the matter wae you? (Billy goes berserk) Jamie, help me! Haud him doon.

JAMIE: Come on, Billy. Its over! Ye hid a dream. Its over.

BILLY: Ah've goat him oan me. Some of him went oan me. Get him aff me!

EDDY: Jesus, Billy. Ah didnae think you'd be the furst tae crack, man. Ah thoat you'd be the last tae go. (Eddy cannot watch this. He goes back to his bunk and sits with his head in his hands).
BILLY: Ah'm losin it. Ah'm losin it. (Sitting up, rocking, shivering, and cuddling himself).

JAMIE: Yer awright! Yer awright! (To Eddy, nodding at the empty bunk) Gie me ower that jaicket!

EDDY: (Looking away, hands Jamie the jacket) Here.

JAMIE: (Putting the dead man's jacket round Billy's shoulders) Here. Pit this roon ye. Yer awright. (Sits beside him, arm round his shoulder).

BILLY: We never even knew his name. We never even fun oot his name!

JAMIE: It's over an done wae.

BILLY: Ah'm sorry! Ah'm sorry!

EDDY: (Not looking at Billy) Ye've nothin tae be sorry fur.

JAMIE: We're yer pals. We're right beside ye.

BILLY: We should've stoapped them. We jist stood there an let them dae it.

JAMIE: Its over. Its history. There wiz nothin we could dae.

EDDY: (Turning round) We wur none of us tae blame! (Sits on the other side of Billy).

BILLY: (Calmer now) Ah'm sorry.

[The three men lean against one another. There is a long silence. Lights out].

Scene 16: Daily Worker

Glasgow Green, July 1937.

[Lights up. A Communist Party member stands on a wooden platform, waving papers, and haranguing the audience].

DAILY WORKER: Get yer 'Daily Worker'! Read aw aboot the war in Spain! Thousands killed bae Hitler's bombs! The British Government pursues a gutless policy ae appeasement! Read the stories ye don't get in the bosses' papers! See pictures ae the International Brigade in action. Support the Popular Front Government, the Government ae aw anti-fascists! Only united mass action can save the Spanish Republic! Arms for Spain! Defeat Fascism! The Communist Party calls upon aw anti-fascists tae defend Spanish democracy. Hundreds ae oor members hiv already made the supreme sacrifice. Thegither we can brek fascism in Spain an stoap the disease spreading. International workin class solidarity is whit Franco, Hitler, and Mussolini fear maist. They depend oan the spinelessness ae Westminster fur victory. The Labour Movement in Glasgow has a great responsibility. Labour must act now! Organise the fight against fascism! End the fiasco ae non-intervention! Bring doon Chamberlain! Support the heroic International Brigade ae the Spanish Republican Army! Don't let them stand alone! Victory tae the Spanish Republic! No Pasaran!

[Lights out].

Scene 17: Still Life

Green's Cinema, July 1937.

[Mary Collins is pacing up and down with her torch. Mr Thomson is setting up the projector to show her the news bulletin].

MARY: Gonnae get a move oan, you. Ah know it's him. He's in here somewhere.

MR THOMSON: (Fidgeting with the lens) Oh for goodness sake, woman, stop harassing me while I'm doing this. It's a tricky business, you know.

MARY: Jist let me see ma boay again.

MR THOMSON: There. All set. Now we'll see what's what and who's who.

[The film runs. We see news from around the world, then images of the war in Spain flicker on the screen].

MARY: Ah knew it wisnae him. (Tearfully, tugging at her hair) Somethin's wrang. Somethin's happened tae ma Jamie.

[The film finishes. Lights out].

Scene 18: The Great Escape

Salamanca, July 1937.

[Billy is on his bunk, scratching, sweating, and looking bored. Jamie is sitting beside Eddy, teaching him to read. Billy feels left out].

BILLY: Emdy want tae test thur strength, then?

EDDY: Whit hiv ye goat in mind?

BILLY: (Kneeling beside the table, placing his elbow on it, fist raised) Come on. Who's preperd tae take oan Big Billy Biceps, the man wae the stroangest forearm in the Parkhead Forge?

EDDY: Well seen how you pass yur time.

JAMIE: (Walks over to the table, wiping his hands on his trousers) Awright, granda. Ah'll take ye oan.

EDDY: (Joining them) Ah'll be the referee.

BILLY: Dae ye know the rules?

JAMIE: (Getting into position) Furst haun tae touch the table is the loser's.

BILLY: Right. (To Eddy) When yer ready.

EDDY: Oan the count a three. Wan. Two. Three!

[Billy and Jamie begin to struggle. The strain shows first on Jamie, his arm bending back as Billy puts all his power into one big push, but gradually Jamie forces his arm upright again. The two men sweat it out for half a minute, then Billy slams Jamie's arm down on the table with a loud crack. Jamie lets out a howl].

EDDY: Jesus, Billy! Ye coulda broke his bloody haun there.

BILLY: (Getting to his feet, red-faced, sweating, angry) Ah've a good mind tae brek his bloody neck! He wiz diggin his nails right intae ma haun, the wee bastard! Look! (Shows Eddy the back of his hand).

EDDY: Ah'd kiss it better, but ah know where it's been.

JAMIE: (Cradling his arm against his chest) Is it ma fault ah've no hid a manicure?

BILLY: Ah'll fuckin manicure ye!

[Eddy has gone round behind Billy and now goes down on all fours. Jamie looks up and sees the opportunity. He struggles to his feet, holding out his good hand].

JAMIE: Sorry aboot the nails, big man. Nae hard feelins, eh?

BILLY: (Leers at him for a moment, then holds out his hand and shakes with Jamie) Yer no ready tae take oan a real man yet, young yin.

[Jamie pulls his hand free and gives Billy a gentle push in the chest, sending him tumbling over Eddy's back, and crashing to the floor. Billy rolls over, gets up and charges at Eddy as he gets to his feet. Jamie sticks out a leg and Billy goes down again. Eddy pulls a red handkerchief from his shirt pocket. Jamie picks up a stool. Like the three stooges, the men go round and round, Eddy and Jamie playing the bullfighters to Billy's raging bull. Finally, Billy charges both his cellmates, they sidestep, and he goes over the dead man's bunk. Eddy and Jamie hold their sides in silent mirth].

BILLY: (Standing up and dusting himself off. Then, as though nothing had happened) Wur missin the Fair, ye know. Hauf a Glasgow'll be headin fur the coast. (Pacing up and down) Ah should be in Saltcoats, no Salamanca. Who knows. Mibbe wan day we'll aw be gaun tae Spain fur wur holidays. Ah, bit gie me Glesca any day. The moarnin mist risin oan the Green. The smell a the Barras oan a Sunday efternin. A few boattles a stout by the Clyde an watchin the sun go doon. (Billy starts to sing in an exaggerated Music Hall turn, swaggering in front of Eddy and Jamie)
     I sing of a river I'm happy beside
     The song that I sing is the song of the Clyde
     Of all Scottish rivers its dearest to me
     It flows from Leadhills all the way to the sea.

EDDY: Gaun yersel!

JAMIE: Wan singer wan song!

[Billy then goes into Harry Lauder routine, singing 'Ah belang tae Glesca'. Eddy and Jamie clap when he finishes].

EDDY: Ah take it yer homesick?

BILLY: A bit.

EDDY: Me tae. Many's the time ah've asked masel jist whit the hell ah'm daein here. Ah mean ah got bullied bae lassies when ah wiz a wee boay. Ahm jist no cut oot tae be a soldier.

BILLY: It's no exactly a vocation yer born tae. Anyway that's why the gun wiz invented. So ye didnae need tae fight sumdy man-tae-man. Ye could jist shoot them fae twinty yards away an call yersel a hero.

EDDY: Ah don't think ah could shoot sumdy fae twinty inches away. Ma aim's terrible. Ma ma wiz always checkin me fur peein ower the lavvy pan.

BILLY: We'll need tae find somethin else fur ye tae dae then. Mibbe ye could write a new communist manifesto. Wance ye learn tae write that is. By the way, how's the lessons comin alang?

JAMIE: Gie it a bye, you.

BILLY: Ma apologies tae the great socialist teacher. John MacLean eat yer heart oot. Bit that gie's me an idea you guys. You could write a polite wee letter tae Franco askin him tae wise up an let us oot a this fleapit. Ahm sure he'll be impressed bae the effort yiz pit intae it. "Hey mister, gonnae gie us oor baw back."

JAMIE: Ah think ah'll go daft if ah've got tae spend another night in here.

BILLY: Wid ye know the difference?

JAMIE: Yiv got too much time tae think aboot things in here. Ah cannae wait tae get back tae Glasgow. Ma mammy ay said ye don't know how much ye love Glasgow tae yer miles away fae hame. She's no been further than Adrossan right enough.

BILLY: Adrossan eh? Move over Christopher Columbus. Yer maw must be Shettleston's answer tae Marco Polo. Did she plant a flag in the sand dunes?

JAMIE: Ah love the seaside.

BILLY: Ye shoulda brought yer bucket an spade young yin. Ma wee cousin went tae Moscow wae the Young Communist League. They went tae the Kremlin tae see Stalin. Bit he wiznae in.

JAMIE: That wiz awfy rude a him. Mibbe he wiz in Adrossan. Paintin the town red. (At this point Eddy gets ready to step in, then groans and changes his mind) See me. Ah'm gonnae get ma arse oot a here furst chance ah get.

BILLY: Whit's the point? They're movin us next week.

JAMIE: Movin us ma arse. No way ah'm ah gonnae sit here an let them gie me a bullet in the back a the heid. Next time they let us oot in that yerd ah'm off. Ah'm tellin ye. Ah'm ower that fence lik a fuckin ferret.

EDDY: Don't even attempt it, Jamie. They've a machine gun trained oan that fence. Cut ye in hauf, so they wull. Even if ye did get ower it. Where wid ye go? Wur slap bang in the middle a naewhere.

JAMIE: Ah'll go somewhere.

BILLY: Bit where?

JAMIE: Ah'll blaw up that bridge when ah come tae it.

BILLY: Jist sit it oot, son. Sit tight. That's the only way tae get through this thing. They'll shoot ye doon lik a dug. Ah'm tellin ye. Yer no in the pictures noo. There's...

JAMIE: Ah know! There's a war oan. Bit we might as well be in Barlinnie fur aw the good we're daein stuck in here...

EDDY: Don't furget why we came, Jamie, an why we're here.

BILLY: Aye, son. We came because we hid eyes tae see an legs tae cerry us. We came tae fight Franco. An we came tae fight fascism. Bit its no jist a matter a who yer fightin, or whit yer fightin. It's who yer fightin fur. Aye, an whit yer fightin fur.

JAMIE: Stuck in here, wur only fightin among wurselves. Oh, fur the sight of a red flag flappin in the breeze. Aye, an a forest a fists raised in defiance!

EDDY: Another week, Jamie. Wan mer week. Haud oan.

JAMIE: They'll bury us in another week.

BILLY: Jamie!

JAMIE: That's the furst time ye've cawd me by my name.

BILLY: Don't let it be the last, then.

JAMIE: Ah'm tellin ye. Ma mind's made up. This is ma last day in this pit. Ah'm sick a stewin in ma ain juice.

BILLY: You're gaun naewhere, son, even if ah hiv tae staun oan yer heid tae stoap ye.

EDDY: (To Jamie) Aye. An me up oan his shooders tae!

BILLY: (To Jamie, emphatically) Ah'm tellin ye. Yer stayin put. Zat right, Eddy? (He shoves Jamie to the floor).

EDDY: Too fuckin right.

JAMIE: (To Billy) Ah'm glad tae see you're back tae yer auld sel.

BILLY: Really?

JAMIE: Aye. Ah preferred ye as a bastard.

[Lights out. Jamie's mother appears, torch in hand].

MARY: (Looking up) Ye've goat tae laugh it them up ther. Aw sich big men. They've goat the world sewn up in an hoor an a hauf.

JAMIE: (Coughing) Ah'm dyin.

MARY: (Flashing her light at him) Ah hear ye, son.

[Lights out].

Scene 19: The Final Curtain

The Necropolis, September 1937.

[Mary and Ann sit on a bench in the cemetery].

ANN: Mammy. How come they didnae bring his boady back?

MARY: Ye know how proud yer brother wiz ae his boady. Never away fae that mirror in the lobby. Efter he went away ah used tae see him in it. Whit a picture!

ANN: Jist tae hiv seen him again.

MARY: Its hard tae believe ah'll no see ma Jamie come roon that coarner at the tap a the street again, whistlin, his hauns in his poackits an his bunnet shoved back oan his heid.

ANN: Ah still watch fur him at the windae.

MARY: Yer da aye thoat Jamie wid end up playin centre forward fur Celtic. Ah mind lookin doon intae the back an seein him playin keepy-up, his wee face that serious. Ah think he tried tae stick in at it efter his faither died bit his heart jist wisnae in it.

ANN: (Playing Jamie, bouncing a ball) Mammy, ah scored a hat trick! Wan a flyin heider! Wan wae ma left fit!

MARY: Look at yer shins, Jamie! Every colour a the rainbow!

ANN: It's the other team mammy. Thur wiz a big hacker oan the right-wing.

MARY: Thur always is.

ANN: Can ah get a piece, ma? Ah'm starvin.

MARY: Away hame an make it yersel. Yer faither's in. Bit wash they manky hauns furst... An he wiz daft aboot the pictures, wiz Jamie. Hurrah fur Hollywood. Tae me it wiz jist a joab. Sick tae death ae the pictures, so ah am. You like them, daen't ye hen?

ANN: Aye mammy.

MARY: Ah used tae like the matinees oan a Seterday. The weans went mental an there wiz aye sweetie papers everywhere. Stampin their feet whenever there wiz a kiss ur an excitin bit. Poor wee mites. Pit them oot their misery fur a while. Kept the world away fur an efternin.

ANN: Jamie says he wiz gonnae be in the pictures an buy me a big fur coat an smoke cigars.

MARY: He could hiv been up there oan that big screen, hen. Aw that life an they good looks gone tae waste. (She fixes her hair and pouts).

ANN: (Looking up at her mother) Mammy! Its Jamie Collins, the famous film star! Aw Mr Collins, ah've seen aw yer films. Gonnae gie me yer autograph.

MARY: (Playing Jamie, Americanised) Sure sweetie. (She pretends to take flowers from Ann) Are these for me?

ANN: Ah saw ye fightin that big gorilla, dancin wae Ginger Rogers, kissin Garbo, fencin wae John Barrymore. Oh, an see when ye wur Dracula an ye bit that wummin's neck, ah nearly choked oan ma sugarolly watter.

MARY: Sugarolly watter, as black as the lum,
Gather up peens, an you'll get some.

MARY: (Still as Jamie, patting Ann's head) Cute kid.

ANN: (Clasping her hands and sighing) Gee, he's swell! (Turning to her mother) Mammy? Whit ah'm ah gonnae be when ah grow up?

MARY: (Back to herself) A wummin, hen, jist lik me. Whit else could ye be?

[Cut to Barcelona, September 1938. Dolores Ibarruri - La Pasionaria - stands centre-stage. Behind her the red and black flags, and the banners of the International Brigade, are waved in the wind].

LA PASIONARIA: You came to us from all peoples, from all places. You came like brothers of ours, like sons of undying Spain; and in the hardest days of the war, when the capital of the Spanish Republic was threatened, it was you, gallant Comrades of the International Brigades, who helped to save the city with your fighting enthusiasm, your heroism and your spirit of sacrifice. In deathless verses Jarama and Guadalajara, Brunete and Belchite, Levante and the Ebro sing the courage, the self-sacrifice, the daring, the discipline of the men of the International Brigades. For the first time in the history of the Peoples' struggles, there has been the spectacle, breath-taking in its grandeur, of the formation of International Brigades to help save a threatened country's freedom and independence, the freedom and independence of our Spanish Land.

[Cut back to Ann and Mary].

ANN: Ah want tae be lik Jamie!

MARY: Naw, no Jamie. Jamie! (Agitated) How did he die? Where did he faw? Wiz it quick? Wiz it slow? God grant him rest wherever he lies. Ah'll never look him in the eyes again.

[Jamie runs on stage in a repeat of the opening scene. Shots ring out. He falls].

ANN: Is that the film finished, mammy?

MARY: Aye, hen. Its aw ower an done wae noo. (She gets up, lifts a coat from the bench, covers Jamie with it, and strokes his hair). Here, son. Yer daddy's coat'll keep ye warm. Yer mammy's here noo. Go back tae sleep. Coory in noo. There's nane a us died a winter yet. Ther ther. Nightie night.

ANN: (Kneels over Jamie, hands clasped, eyes closed, then stands up and takes her mother's hand) Can ah sleep wae you the night, mammy? Jamie's bed's too cauld.

MARY: Course ye can, hen. We'll coory in thegither.

[They walk off together. La Pasionaria reappears].

LA PASIONARIA: Mothers! Women! When the years pass by and the wounds of war are staunched: when the cloudy memory of the sorrowful, bloody days returns in a present of freedom, love, and well-being; when the feelings of rancour are dying away and when pride in a free country is felt equally by all Spaniards - then speak to your children. Tell them of the International Brigades. Tell them how, coming over seas and mountains, crossing frontiers bristling with bayonets, and watched for by ravening dogs thirsty to tear at their flesh, these men reached our country as Crusaders for freedom. They gave up everything; their loves, their country, home and fortune - fathers, mothers, wives, brothers, sisters and children and they came and told us: "We are here, your cause, Spain's cause, is ours. It is the cause of all advanced and progressive mankind." Today they are going away. Many of them, thousands of them, are staying here with the

Spanish earth for their shroud, and all Spaniards remember them with the deepest feeling.

[Cut to Salamanca. Eddy is reading from Jamie's diary. Billy looks on].

BILLY: "My comrades..."

EDDY: (Slowly, stumbling over the words) "My Comrades, Billy and Eddy, have been like brothers to me..."

BILLY: On ye go...

EDDY: "When this is all over. When the war is won. I can see the three of us. Walking up the High Street, arm in arm, just like brothers. People will point at us and say: 'They're they are. There's the men of the International Brigade...'"

BILLY: Keep gaun.

EDDY: (Wiping his eyes, closing the diary, and handing it to Billy) Naw. You read it. Ah cannae make oot his writin...

[Lights out. Cut to La Pasionaria].

LA PASIONARIA: Comrades of the International Brigades! Political reasons, reasons of State, the welfare of that same cause for which you offered your blood with boundless generosity, are sending you back, some of you to your own countries and others to forced exile. You can go proudly. You are history. You are legend. You are the heroic example of democracy's solidarity and universality. We shall not forget you, and when the olive tree of peace puts forth its leaves again, mingled with the laurels of the Spanish Republic's victory - come back! Come back to us. With us those of you who have no country will find one, those of you who have to live deprived of friendship will find friends, and all of you will find the love and gratitude of the whole Spanish people who, now and in the future, will cry out with all their hearts: "Long live the heroes of the International Brigades!"

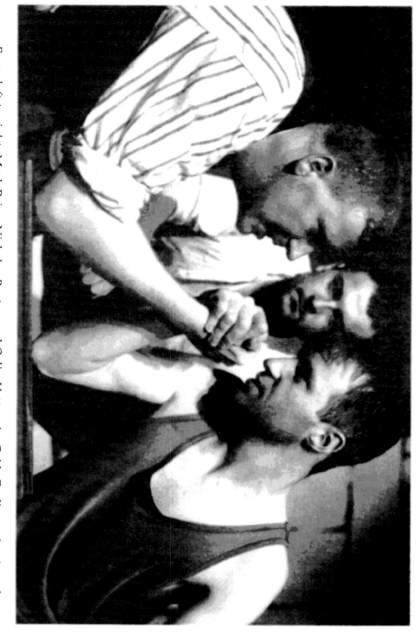

From left to right: Mark Price, Nicholas Beaton and Colin Vetters in Gable End's production of **From the Calton to Catalonia**, *Arches Theatre, November 1991.*

What the critics said...

"Glasgow's contribution to the fight against fascist Spain...celebrated with wit and compassion."

THE EVENING TIMES

"...bristling with energy and intelligence."

THE SCOTSMAN

"...an honest tribute and a commemoration of courage and sacrifice."

THE GLASGOW HERALD

About the authors

JOHN MALEY is a poet and playwright. His poems have been published in **Strata, Hard Lines, New Writing Scotland, Northwest Passages,** and **The Individual Spoke**. His performed plays include **The Furst Fit** (1989), **From the Calton to Catalonia** (1990), and **Gallowglass** (1991), all co-written with Willy Maley. His most recent plays include **The Home Front**, the story of the 1915 rent strikes, and **The Hungry Man**, about the Hunger Marches of the 1930s.

WILLY MALEY is a lecturer, journalist, and playwright. He has had six plays performed at Mayfest. He is author of **Inlaws and Outlaws** (1990), co-author of **The Lions of Lisbon** (1992), and co-author and project co-ordinator of Edinburgh Fringe First Winner **No Mean Fighter** (1992). He is presently working on **Dirt Enters at the Heart**, a play about the spread of AIDS in the prison system, to be performed by CAT A Theatre Company at the 1993 Edinburgh Fringe.

NOTE ON PRODUCTION HISTORY

Mean City (Unlimited) Theatre Company, Lithgow Theatre, Govan, Glasgow, 3-7 December 1990 (Directed by Alex McSherry);

Mean City (Unlimited) Theatre Company, Mayfest 1991 (Directed by Alex McSherry);

Gable End Theatre Company, Scottish Trade Union Week, Arches Theatre, 11-12November 1991 (Directed by Libby McArthur);

West Theatre Company, Diverse Attractions, Edinburgh Fringe Festival, 10-22 August 1992 (Directed by Andrew Hay);

Kayos Theatre Company, Greenock Arts Guild Theatre, 11-12 June 2004 (Directed by Mark Barclay);

Kayos Theatre Company, Tramway Theatre, Glasgow, 1-4 December 2004 (Directed by Mark Barclay); two scenes from the play, 'Food for Spain and 'Boxing Clever', were staged at Mono Cafe Bar as part of Ya Basta! Cabaret Night on Monday 6 June 2005, directed by Mark Barclay and featuring some of the cast from Kayos;

Strathclyde Theatre Group, The Ramshorn Theatre, Glasgow, 26-31 January 2009 (Directed by Kevin Jannetts);

Red Productions, Arts Guild Theatre, Greenock, 4-5 March 2010 (Directed by Keegan Friel);

Basement Theatre Company, Pearce Institute, Govan, Glasgow, 5-7 May2010, and The Wynd, Paisley, 13-14 May 2010 (Directed by Heather Mackenzie).

Copyright rests with the authors. For information on future productions please contact: Willy.Maley@glasgow.ac.uk

If you are not already a member of the International Brigade Memorial Trust, we urge you to join.

The IBMT keeps alive the memory and spirit of the men and women from Britain, Ireland and elsewhere who volunteered to defend democracy and fight fascism in Spain from 1936 to 1939.

International Brigade Memorial Trust

6 Stonells Road
London
SW11 6HQ

020 7228 6504

www.international-brigades.org.uk

ESSENTIAL READING ON THE SPANISH CIVIL WAR

Bill Alexander, *British Volunteers for Liberty: Spain 1936-1939* (Lawrence and Wishart, 1982).

Mike Arnott, *Dundee and the Spanish Civil War* (Dundee: Dundee Trades Union Council, 2008).

Richard Baxell, *British Volunteers in the Spanish Civil War* (Aberschyan: Warren and Pell, 2007).

Antony Beevor, *The Battle for Spain* (London: Weidenfeld & Nicolson, 2006).

Tom Buchanan, *Britain and the Spanish Civil War* (Cambridge: Cambridge University Press, 1997).

Chris Dolan, *An Anarchist's Story: The Life of Ethel MacDonald* (Edinburgh: Birlinn, 2009).

Daniel Gray, *Homage to Caledonia: Scotland and the Spanish Civil War* (Edinburgh: Luath Press, 2008).

Dolores Ibarruri, *They Shall Not Pass: The Autobiography of La Pasionaria* (New York: International Publishers, 1966).

Ian MacDougall, *Voices from the Spanish Civil War: Personal Recollections of Scottish Volunteers in Republican Spain 1936-39* (Edinburgh: Polygon, 1986).

George Orwell, *Homage to Catalonia* (London: Secker and Warburg, 1938).

Paul Preston and Ann Mackenzie (eds.), *The Republic Besieged: Civil War in Spain 1936-1939* (Edinburgh: Edinburgh University Press, 1996).

Paul Preston, *A Concise History of the Spanish Civil War* (London: Fontana Press, London, 1996).

Paul Preston, *Comrades!: Portraits from the Spanish Civil War* (London: HarperCollins, 1999).

Paul Preston, *Doves of War: Four Women of Spain* (London: Harper Collins, 2002).

Paul Preston, *The Spanish Civil War: Reaction, Revolution and Revenge* (London: Harper Perennial, 2006).

Paul Preston, *We Saw Spain Die: Foreign Correspondents in the Spanish Civil War* (London: Constable and Robinson, 2008).

Paul Preston, *The Spanish Holocaust: Inquisition and Extermination in Twentieth-Century Spain* (London: HarperPress, 2012).

@CaltonBooks

www.calton-books.co.uk

If you are in Glasgow why not visit our shop?

We are located less than 15 minutes walk from Glasgow Cross.

Here you will find a wide selection of new & pre-loved books, t-shirts, badges, flags, cd's & more. Including a wide-range of merchandise on the Spanish civil war.

GLASGOW'S INDEPENDENT RADICAL BOOKSHOP

159 LONDON RD GLASGOW G1 5BX
shop@calton-books.co.uk   tel: 07590 262 987

follow us on facebook